20th Century Defences
in the West Midlands

20th Century Defences
in the West Midlands

Colin Jones, Bernard Lowry and Mick Wilks

Logaston Press

LOGASTON PRESS
Little Logaston Woonton Almeley
Herefordshire HR3 6QH
logastonpress.co.uk

Published 2008

ISBN 978 1904396 99 4

Typeset by Logaston Press
and printed in Great Britain by
Bell & Bain Ltd, Glasgow

Front cover: A sculpture outside the Castle Bromwich factory which produced
Spitfires in the Second World War. The sculpture is on a roundabout on the
Heartlands Spine Road at the eastern end of the factory, which is now owned
by Jaguar.

Contents

Acknowledgments

Our grateful thanks to Dr Mike Osborne who suggested this book and provided invaluable help; to Malcolm Atkin and the staff of Worcestershire Historic Environment and Archaeological Service (WHEAS) for their help over many years; to Steve Carvell for allowing us to use his information on Warwickshire; to Dr Ernest Putley and Don Tomlin for their help on radar in Worcestershire; to Alan Smith of Staffordshire Fire and Rescue Service; to Armand De Fillipo of the Shropshire Record Office; to Charles Purcell of the Bewdley Historical Research Group; to Ron Henry, Joe Hurley and Keith Trafford (all ex TRE/RRE); to the late Geoff Roberts (ex CAAEE); to the staffs of the former Army Medal Office at Droitwich, of RHQ/WFR, Norton Barracks, of both the Herefordshire and Worcestershire Record Offices, and of the former Army Technical Services Agency at Pale Manor; to Dr John Schofield of English Heritage; to Adrian Armishaw; to Wayne Cocroft; to Brian Heatley; and lastly, but not least, to our wives Sylvia, Geraldine and Vicky for their forbearance whilst we laboured on this book.

Glossary

AA	Anti-Aircraft
AAOR	Anti-Aircraft Operations Room
ABL	American British Laboratory (linked with Massachusetts Institute of Technology)
ADEE	Air Defence Experimental Establishment
ADRDE	Army Defence Research & Development Establishment
AFS	Auxiliary Fire Service
AI	Airborne Interception
AMRE	Air Ministry Research Establishment
ARP	Air Raid Precautions
ASV	Air to Surface Vessel
AT	Anti-tank
ATS	Auxiliary Territorial Service
BBRL	British Based Radiation Laboratory (linked with Harvard University)
BEF	British Expeditionary Force
Breastwork	An above ground, breast-high defence work often built of sandbags. Used in low-lying and waterlogged areas. Also referred to as 'parapet'.
'Brownfield Sites'	Previously developed land, including redundant defence sites, targeted by planners for new developments.
BRS	Bawdsey Research Station
BSA	Birmingham Small Arms Co
CAAEE	Coastal Artillery & Anti-Aircraft Experimental Establishment
CAD	Central Ammunition Depot
COD	Central Ordnance Depot
CWGC	Commonwealth War Graves Commission
defra	Department for Environment, Food & Rural Affairs
DERA	Defence Electronics Research Agency
DoB	Defence of Britain Project
DRA	Defence Research Agency
'Eureka'	A portable, ground-based electronic beacon

FANY	First Aid Nursing Yeomanry
Flame Fougasse	A rudimentary anti-tank device, utilising one or more 40 gallon barrels of flammable liquid set in a roadside bank. Each device would project a flame across the road and would be ignited by a remotely controlled small explosive charge set behind each barrel.
FW3	Fortifications and Works No. 3, a branch of the War Office Directorate of Fortifications and Works which was responsible for the design of many pillboxes.
GCHQ	Government Communications Headquarters
GCI	Ground Controlled Interception
GDA	Gun Defended Area
Gee and Gee-H	Electronic navigation systems utilising beams radiated from ground-based transmitters.
GHQ	General Headquarters
GHQ Line	A major Second World War defence line, about 50 miles inland of the south and east coasts linking London and Bristol and running up to Edinburgh.
GPO	General Post office
HAA	Heavy anti-aircraft (artillery)
HG	Home Guard
'H$_2$S'	An aircraft mounted, downward scanning radar system used for bombing target identification in cloudy conditions or in darkness.
ID	Infantry Division (US)
Kinetheodolite	Optical instrument with movie camera for tracking airborne objects
LAA	Light anti-aircraft (artillery)
LDV	Local Defence Volunteers
Link Trainer	An indoor device to simulate flying an aircraft and, specifically at TRE, airborne radar operating systems in order to practise techniques before airborne trials were undertaken.
LMS	London, Midland & Scottish Railway
Meacon	Masking Beacon
Molotov Cocktail	A glass bottle filled with petrol and with a rag fuse that was ignited immediately before the bottle was thrown at a target.
MT	Motor Transport
MU	Maintenance Unit
NATO	North Atlantic Treaty Organisation

'Nickels'	RAF operations involving the dropping of propaganda leaflets over enemy territory.
Nissen hut	Military accommodation hut of corrugated, curved steel sections.
Nodal Point	A military term to describe a defended urban area around an important road and/or rail junction. Also see entry for 'Stud' System below.
'Oboe'	A ground transmitter system to supplement 'Gee' and used for allied bomber target marking.
OCTU	Officer Cadet Training Unit (Army)
Orlit Post	Small, pre-fabricated structure used on early postwar ROC Posts
OTU	Operational Training Unit (RAF)
PLUTO	Pipeline underwater transport of oil. (Note: Often referred to as 'Pipeline under the Ocean' although in reality the pipeline was under the English Channel.)
PoW	Prisoner of War
Pravda	Official Soviet newspaper
PWE	Political Warfare Executive
QAIMNS	Queen Alexandra's Imperial Military Nursing Service
RA	Royal Artillery
'Radar'	An American term, now in general use, derived from **Ra**dio **D**irection **A**nd **R**anging. Prior to the Second World War the British used the term 'RDF', Radio Direction Finding, to help disguise the purpose of the equipment.
'Ranger'	Freelance RAF fighter intrusion operations.
RAOC	Royal Army Ordnance Corps
RASC	Royal Army Service Corps
RAP	Regimental Aid Post
RDF	Radio Direction Finding
'Rebecca'	The airborne element of 'Eureka'
REME	Royal Electrical & Mechanical Engineers
RLG	Relief Landing Ground
RN	Royal Navy
RNAD	Royal Navy Armaments Depot
ROC	Royal Observer Corps
ROF	Royal Ordnance Factory
'Rotor'	Name given to programme to modernise the UK's radar defences in the early 1950s
RRE	Radar Research Establishment
RRFU	Radar Research Flying Unit
RSG	Regional Seat of Government

SAS	Special Air Service
Shadow factory	Factories set up before the Second World War in anticipation of the military demands of the coming war. They 'shadowed' major factories located in areas vulnerable to bombing.
SLG	Satellite Landing Ground
SOE	Special Operations Executive
STC	Senior Training Corps
'Stud' System	System adopted in the middle of the war whereby sections of the Home Guard were grouped to defend particular areas. The largest were known as 'anti-tank islands' which might encompass a whole town; with larger defended areas, such as a conurbation, protected by a group of often mutually supporting 'centres of resistance'; or in the case of smaller defended areas, such as bridges, known as 'defended localities'.
TA	Territorial Army
TFU	Telecommunications Flying Unit
TOB	Temporary Office Building
TRE	Telecommunications Research Establishment
UKWMO	United Kingdom Warning & Monitoring Organisation
USAAF	United States Army Air Force
VAD	Voluntary Aid Detachment
V-bomber	Valiant, Victor & Vulcan Bombers
V1	German Flying Bomb
V2	German Long-range Rocket
VI	Voluntary Interceptor
'Vitguard'	Formalised Home Guard, mid-war system for the guarding and defending of vital or vulnerable points such as factories, telephone exchanges.
VP	Vulnerable Point
VTC	Voluntary Training Corps
WAAF	Women's Auxiliary Air Force
WHEAS	Worcestershire Historic Environment and Archaeology Service
'Window'	A British radar jamming system utilising strips of aluminium foil dropped from aircraft.
WLA	Women's Land Army
WU	Wireless Unit
WVS (later WRVS)	Women's (Royal) Voluntary Service
Y-Service	Name given to wireless interception
Z Battery	Multiple Static AA Rocket Launchers
Zeppelin	German First World War Airship

Introduction

Only in the last few years has any real interest been shown in military and civil defence structures of the twentieth century other than by specialist enthusiasts. These latter have usually belonged to organisations such as the Fortress Study Group (FSG), the Pillbox Study Group (PSG) and the Airfield Research Group. In 1995, following a pilot study in Holderness by the FSG, the Defence of Britain Project (DoB) was set up to identify and record twentieth century military and civil defence structures across the United Kingdom. This also involved most of the major heritage organisations and a large number of volunteers, who submitted records to a central database which can now be found on the internet (http://ads.ahds.ac.uk/catalogue/specColl/dob/). The DoB project ended in 2002 although some volunteers (which includes the authors) have continued their researches. Additionally, much good work on cold war sites has been undertaken by Subterranea Britannica as can be seen on their website www.subbrit.org.uk.

What became apparent from the various reports submitted was the large quantity of structures that had already disappeared and the numbers still disappearing. After the First World War defence structures were rapidly removed as it was thought that that war was the war to end all wars. In 1945 many structures had to be quickly removed as they often occupied road space – air raid shelters and emergency water tanks are prime examples. Also many were on what we would now call brownfield sites and the land was needed for new housing and factories. This process has accelerated following the end of the Cold War in 1989. Time has taken its toll of other structures which have crumbled with age. This book highlights the various types of structures and gives examples of those that survive (or did when the book was completed in the autumn of 2007). It is the hope of the authors that some examples of structures will be given statutory protection and retained as part of our national heritage.

This book, one of a series originating from the DoB Project, gives brief descriptions of the various types of defence structures in the West Midlands and lists examples that can still be seen, most of which are in the more rural areas which have not been subject to redevelopment. The West Midlands has for most of the twentieth century been an important UK industrial base. As such it has heavily supported the military machine through its production facilities which included munitions and aircraft. The presence of these facilities, particularly during the Second World War, meant that this area needed to be heavily defended and, concomitantly, was targeted by German bombers. Parts of the West Midlands are important agricultural areas and became even more so when food supplies were short in both wars. Additionally this area in the Second World War was chosen as a base for the royal family and the government should London have become untenable due to bombing or a German invasion. Some parts of the government did in fact move to the area. The area was also important in the Second World War because the development of radar continued in Worcestershire after the scientists were moved from the vulnerable south coast. Training airfields were located in the area because of its distance from the coasts and thus reasonably secure from attacks by enemy fighters. Finally, it housed many US troops prior to D-Day and many of the hospitals for the casualties after the invasion.

No doubt there are other defence structures surviving in the West Midlands of which the authors are unaware. We would be delighted to be informed of such sites so that they can be recorded for posterity.

In the main the sites listed in this book can be seen from public rights of way. If they are on private land then the permission of the land owner should be sought before entry to his land. Even then care should be taken as the sites can be dangerous after 60+ years.

Other titles in the series are:
'Kent' by D Burridge and 'Lincolnshire' by M Osborne. Both published by Brasseys in 1997
'Cambridgeshire' by M Osborne published by Concrete Publications in 2001
'The East Midlands' by M Osborne published by Concrete Publications in 2003
'The London Area' by M Osborne published by Concrete Publications in 2007

WAR PRODUCTION AND STORAGE

Introduction

Demand for military supplies of all descriptions obviously increases considerably in time of war and often these supplies can only be provided by local (i.e. UK) production. In both world wars the military demand resulted in government control of industry. In the First World War this only covered certain industries, whereas in the Second such control was all-embracing. In the period 1940-1945, unless a factory was providing essentials for the home market, it was involved in production for the military. As well as factories, motor repair garages and even some farm buildings were used for war production. At the end of the Second World War such controls ended and any procurement for the Cold War was done by the placing of orders with either government bodies or private industry.

The movement of war stores and troops in the Second World War required an enlargement of the railway system as this was then the main form of internal transport. New spurs and stations were built and old lines resurrected. A new form of signal box, the so-called ARP model, more fire and blast proof than the existing models, was designed. Remote, emergency signal systems in protected buildings provided a back-up for important railway junctions.

Munitions

Immediately prior to 1914 there were three Royal Ordnance Factories – Enfield, Waltham Abbey and Woolwich. In addition to these, small arms ammunition was produced by a number of private companies mainly in the Birmingham area. The onset of the First World War resulted in a massive increase in demand for ammunition and shells. The initial failure to meet this demand resulted in the infamous shell shortage problem in the spring of 1915. To overcome this, a Ministry of Munitions was set up with Lloyd George as the minister and an extensive programme was started to build a number of national factories for the three stages of production – producing the case, producing the explosive and, finally, filling the case with the explosive. In the West Midlands new factories were located at Hereford (filling), Coventry (filling), Oldbury (explosives) and at Worcester (small arms ammunition). Hereford was also used for the filling of mustard gas shells. A factory for producing acetone (used in cordite production) was built at Ludlow but was not completed until after the end of the war and so was not used. After 1919 the government disposed of many of the national factories but Hereford (Rotherwas) and part of the Worcester (Blackpole) site were retained as reserve factories. As well as the ROFs and the existing private producers, other

1/1 Part of what was the ROF at Worcester. (Colin Jones)

1/2 Entrance to one of the underground storage facilities at ROF, Swynnerton, Staffordshire. (Tom Lowry)

companies like Villiers of Wolverhampton also produced ammunition during the First World War.

The production of rifles before 1914 was shared between the Birmingham Small Arms (BSA) factories in Birmingham and the ROF at Enfield. Virtually all of the larger guns were made by private industry with machine guns being produced by BSA and by Hotchkiss at Coventry. These continued into the First World War but, because of increased demand, in 1917 a National Machine Gun Factory was established at Burton-on-Trent. The only factory in the West Midlands producing larger guns was the Coventry Ordnance Works, which had closed by 1925.

Until 1935 there were only the three pre-1914 ROFs in operation but by 1939 another ten had been approved and by 1942 there were about 40 in operation (this number included engineering ROFs that produced guns and shell cases). Included in these numbers were Hereford and Worcester which had been brought back into production, as well as Featherstone and Swynnerton (Staffs), and Summerfield,

near Kidderminster (Worcs). In addition to these many factories in the West Midlands were involved in the making of cartridge and shell cases. All these new factories, apart from Summerfield, ceased production at the end of or soon after 1945. As well as the ROFs much munitions work was undertaken by private companies under ROF direction. One such company was Cadbury's at Bourneville who had part of their factory turned over to munitions work.

As with munitions it was not till 1935 that thought was given to the extension of production of all types of guns if there was to be another war. In 1938 BSA began producing machine guns at their factory in Small Heath. During the war BSA was to occupy over 30 sites in the West Midlands producing rifles, sub-machine guns and machine guns. Also ICI at Witton was producing small arms. Although there were no assemblers of large field guns in the West Midlands many firms were involved in the production of gun parts. In the main these would have been engineering and

1/3 Some of the remaining buildings of the ROF, Featherstone, Staffordshire. (Colin Jones)

1/4 The main entrance of the First World War administration building of ROF, Rotherwas, Hereford. As can be seen, the building has been renovated by the current owners. (Colin Jones)

similar companies who had the necessary skills and machinery for this type of production and included some of the carpet firms in Kidderminster. The Sentinel Waggon Co at Shrewsbury produced hundreds of Bren Gun Carriers.

An important contribution to the war effort was the removal of most of the operations of the large and vulnerable Woolwich Arsenal complex, east of London, to a new site at Donnington near Wellington in Shropshire in the summer of 1939. The new Central Ordnance Depot stored guns and other military hardware, as well as assembling equipment, much of the latter work being carried out by women. To house the new and evacuated workforce a number of camps as well as over 800 houses were built. The site remains in use.

In the Cold War Summerfield was used for the production of rocket motors and fuel, as was the Armstrong Siddeley factory at Ansty in Warwickshire.

Aircraft

Prior to the First World War the production of aircraft was very much an infant industry and involved approximately ten firms, none of which had been in operation for more than two years. During the war output of aircraft expanded exponentially from less than 1,000 a year before 1914 to about 30,000 in 1918. Factories that had previously not built aircraft were turned over to their production, one such being the Austin factory at Longbridge which had been constructed to manufacture cars. Another such factory was that owned by Armstrong Siddeley at Parkside, Coventry, which started producing aircraft and engines in 1915. The Birmingham Carriage Co at Smethwick also produced aircraft. Aero engines were made by Sunbeam, who also went on to build aircraft, and by Clyno at Wolverhampton. Other local companies made aircraft parts, one example being Brinton's at Kidderminster. The car companies at Coventry were also involved in the production of aircraft and engines.

After the war aircraft production was heavily scaled back with the demand for military aircraft, such as it was, being the

1/5 Part of Castle Bromwich Spitfire and Lancaster factory. (Colin Jones)

mainstay of what remained of the industry. As with munitions it was not till 1935 that thought was given to the need for aircraft for a future war. In 1936 the concept of 'shadow' factories was announced by the government. These were to be factories that would be designated for the production of aircraft and parts if a war started. Initially it was envisaged that they would be managed on an agency basis by engineering firms and in particular the car companies. This was later extended to management by the aircraft firms themselves. Initially firms wanted to construct the shadow factory next to their current premises but later there was pressure to erect them away from the major towns to reduce the chance of the factories being bombed. Morris Motors erected a shadow factory at Castle Bromwich for the construction of aircraft. From 1940 onwards the factory was managed by Vickers Armstrong. Initially the factory produced Spitfires but from 1943 onwards it produced Avro Lancaster bombers. In a rural area Morgan Crucible

1/6 The remains of the shadow factory at Peaton, Shropshire. (Colin Jones)

4

erected a shadow factory at Norton (near Worcester); Garrington's at Bromsgrove was also a shadow factory. There was another rural shadow factory at Peaton in Shropshire which produced aircraft fuel tanks.

The advent of heavy bombing resulted in the construction of underground shadow factories early in the war. At Longbridge a complete factory for aircraft production was built under the existing factory, and at Drakelow (north Worcs) an underground factory was built for the production of aero engines parts. Another underground factory was to be built in the caverns under Dudley Castle but was never used as such because construction took too long. Drakelow later found use

1/7 One of the entrances to the underground shadow factory at Drakelow in Worcestershire. (Mick Wilks)

as a Regional Seat of Government (RSG) (see chapter 9).

As well as the planning for shadow factories, from 1936 onwards discussions took place with the car manufacturers about their producing aircraft if war was declared. Consequently, from 1939 onwards all the car manufacturers took on aircraft production as well as in many cases continuing to produce military vehicles. Longbridge produced aircraft again, as they did in the First World War, and had their own airfield so that the completed aircraft could be flown out. After the war the airfield site was used for the construction of new factory buildings. The car factories at Coventry were turned over to making aero engines and parts. At Baginton (near Coventry) a new factory had been opened by Armstrong Siddeley to produce aircraft (this factory closed in 1965) whilst engines were produced at Parkside (this latter factory closed in 1995). Aircraft were also assembled at the Armstong Siddeley factory at Ansty (as in the First World War). Rootes produced aircraft at Ryton-on-Dunsmore and, from 1942 onwards, at a new factory at Blythe Bridge (near Stoke on Trent) with the aircraft being towed the short distance to Meir to take off. In addition to the car manufacturers, Boulton Paul produced aircraft at Pendeford, Wolverhampton (the local municipal airport) having moved there in 1936.

Many other companies in the West Midlands were requisitioned by the Ministry of Aircraft Production, which had been set up in 1940, and used for the production of aircraft and aero engine parts. For example, many garages in Shrewsbury, including the Midland Red garage, were involved in making wing parts for Castle Bromwich as was the firm of H.A. Saunders in Worcester. This was part of a policy to disperse production to limit the effects of bombing as early bombing raids had shown how vulnerable parts of the industry were. For example, Rists Ltd moved from Lowestoft, to avoid the bombing of the east coast, to a requisitioned factory in Nuneaton where they produced cables and wiring for aircraft.

Part of the development of the jet engine also took place in the West Midlands. The jet engine was invented by Sir Frank Whittle in the early 1930s and was first developed at the British Thomson-Houston factory in Rugby, with the first test taking place there in 1937. In 1938 development then moved across the county boundary to Lutterworth in Leicestershire. However, due to pressure on space there, rooms were rented for use as offices at Brownsover Hall on the outskirts of Rugby. In 1940 the Air Ministry involved the Rover Company (Coventry) in further development of the engine, but within two years they had passed it over to Rolls Royce who did some of the work at a factory in Newcastle-under-Lyme from 1943 onwards (previously the factory had been used by BSA to produce aircraft cannon). The first British jet fighter in service, the Meteor, flew in 1944 having been produced by the Gloster Aircraft Company. After the war jet engines were developed and produced by Armstrong Siddeley at Ansty (the factory is now part of Rolls Royce).

Other War Materials

During both wars the car manufacturers continued to produce road vehicles of various types for the armed services. Similarly the motor cycle manufacturers such as Enfield at Redditch and BSA at Birmingham produced military motor cycles during the wars. In the First World War motor cycles were also produced by Clyno Engineering at Wolverhampton but this firm was no longer in existence by the Second World War, and neither was the large producer of military ambulances, McNaughts of Worcester. During the Second World War there was a great demand for tanks and many were supplied by English Electric, two of whose factories were at Rugby and Stafford. In Stoke-on-Trent the pottery firms made ceramics and other clay products for various war uses as well as crockery for the armed

1/8 The fuel storage depot at Ripple near Worcester. (Mick Wilks)

forces and for British Restaurants. The range of military supplies required during a war is vast and the range produced in the West Midlands was similarly extensive. Examples are pilots' gloves, uniforms, blankets, jerrycans, bayonets, webbing etc. It is without doubt that the West Midlands played an important role in the war effort and this is why it was heavily bombed by the Germans. However production was spread throughout the region so that air raids would have limited effects, it was also amazing how quickly production could be resumed after a bombing raid.

As well as factory production of war materials there was also voluntary production usually organised by the WVS. Married women and those too old to be involved in war work would knit socks and other items of clothing ('comforts') for the troops which could all be done at home. In other cases a local parish or village hall might be used to meet and produce camouflage nets for the forces.

The area also made an important contribution in the production of coal for power, chemicals etc. Amongst the coalfields in the area, those in North Staffordshire were perhaps the most important; the large mine at Wolstanton, Newcastle-under-Lyme, was considered to be sufficiently important to merit its own decoy site (see Chapter 8) near Keele. The production of steel relied on the output of coalmines and, again, the steelworks at Shelton, close to Wolstanton, was deemed important enough to have its own decoy at Beech.

Another important raw material required both by the military and for war production was petroleum. Whilst this did not originate in the UK, it did need to be transported throughout the country. Early in the war the rivers and canals were used with petroleum being carried in tankers. Large inland storage depots were opened in Ripple (in South Worcestershire), Worcester and Stourport, all served by the River Severn. Further aviation fuel depots were built at Hinton-on-the-Green (Worcs) and Farley (Shrops, in the side of a quarry) which were served by rail. However it was decided to build pipelines to increase the flow, one running from Liverpool to Avonmouth. Construction of this pipeline commenced in November 1941 and was completed by July 1942. It initially followed the River Severn and then went through Shropshire to Liverpool. The depots at Ripple, Worcester and Stourport were then serviced by this pipeline as well as by the tankers. This pipeline and the others

1/9 Pluto pipeline pumping station at Fordhall Farm near Market Drayton in Shropshire. (Bernard Lowry)

that were constructed eventually formed a network connecting with PLUTO, the pipeline laid under the channel to provide fuel to our invading army after D-Day. During the cold war the national pipeline system was maintained and extended as it would be a secure delivery system if there was a nuclear attack.

The depots at Worcester have now gone but the other Worcestershire sites remain; the large tanks covered by grass can still be seen at Ripple. One wonders, though, how much longer they will remain now that the Cold War is long since over. Further north a Pluto pumping station remains at Fordhall, near Market Drayton.

Vital installations required concealment techniques to disguise them from aerial reconnaissance. At Leamington Spa was established the Civil Defence Camouflage Directorate. Over 240 artists, designs and technicians worked at the Regent Hotel and at other sites in the town on camouflage work.

Civilian Supplies

In addition to food (for which see chapter 3), petrol, clothing, soft furnishings and furniture were rationed during the Second World War. Production of these various items had to be limited as the raw materials were in short supply as they were usually imported. Also, as was stated at the start of this chapter, many factories had to be turned over to production of war materials and thus were unable to produce civilian supplies.

Where items were to continue to be made, production was concentrated in a few factories leaving the rest for war material production. Also to save on materials a limited number of 'utility' (i.e. standard) designs were introduced, with the finished product having to carry a 'utility' logo. There were also restrictions on who could have the necessary ration coupons to purchase the non food items and these restrictions tightened as the war progressed. In the case of petrol, by the end of the war the restriction was total as no private motoring was allowed. Although there has been no rationing since 1954 petrol coupons were issued in the 1970s, when there was an oil shortage, but were never used.

Explosives storage

The remoter areas of the West Midlands provided space for the storage of ammunition and explosives and two large Central Ammunition Depots were constructed in the region during the Second World War. The first to open was that at Nesscliffe in Shropshire with 164 storehouses plus accommodation buildings and workshops. Covering 1,800 acres it had the capacity to store 200,000 tons of explosives. Most of the store buildings, which were designed to minimise the effects of any explosion, remain. A disused railway line, the Shropshire and Montgomeryshire Light Railway, was reinstated to carry ammunition to and from the depot. At Kineton in Warwickshire (still in use by the Army) the first ammunition arrived in October 1942 with storage capacity for 150,000 tons in 252 rail-linked explosive storehouses, six of which remain. A smaller storage depot with nineteen storage buildings, originally served by two locomotives and associ-

1/10 The interior of one of the large number of ordnance storage magazines at Nesscliffe in Shropshire. A light railway moved munitions around the site and it is possible to make out the line in the photograph as well as the storage bays. (Bernard Lowry)

ated with the Rotherwas Filling Factory at Hereford, was established at Pontrilas in 1942. Another store associated with Rotherwas was that at Haywood, south of Hereford.

Two Royal Naval Armament Depots (RNAD) were established in the region in the Second World War. The first came in 1939, when the Great Western Railway Company offered the redundant railway tunnel that ran alongside the replacement operational tunnel through the Malvern Hills, to the Admiralty as a potential store for naval explosives. The tunnel had been abandoned in the 1920s as a result of rock falls caused by poor geology, but with suitable strengthening, the provision of concrete floors and a narrow gauge railway to carry the stored materials to and from the main line, the tunnel served the Navy throughout the war for the storage of bombs, shells and mines, many of these items coming from the ROF at Rotherwas, near Hereford. The store was abandoned

at the end of the war and is inaccessible. However it was designated as a vulnerable point (a strategic site needing an armed guard) and accommodation huts for the guard can still be seen at the Colwall end of the tunnel and at Malvern Wells. The former have now been converted to residential use and can be seen behind Colwall Railway Station, while those at Malvern Wells are in commercial use.

Ditton Priors, the second RNAD, was a remote outpost of the main naval store complex at Priddy's Hard in Hampshire. It was established in 1940 as a facility relatively safe from the bombing and risk of invasion on the south coast and used a semi-redundant railway line, the Cleobury Mortimer and Ditton Priors Light Railway, for the movement of ammunition. It was designed to hold 35,000 tons of explosive stores such as mines, torpedoes and naval shells. Ruston and Hornsby diesel locomotives pulled the open-topped wagons. These were safer than steam, especially as there was much *ad hoc* storage along the side of the line. The site was closed by the Navy in 1965, briefly seeing use as a US ammunition dump up to 1967.

The RAF had seen the need for the countrywide underground storage of ammunition and explosives in the 1930s. The Wren's Nest Quarry at Dudley was one site considered but rejected pre-war. Overall the RAF's experience of storage would be far from a happy one. A site at Fauld in Staffordshire, accommodation being in part of a former gypsum quarry, was acquired by the RAF for bomb storage in 1937. It became No 21 MU with a headquarters, workshops, generator house etc. However wartime needs for ever-greater storage, especially with the advent of bombs of up to 4000 lbs capacity, led to the extension of internal space and from 1942 the addition of three surface sites within a 12 miles radius of Fauld. Italian prisoners of war from the nearby Hilton camp were employed on site after the Italian Armistice in 1943. On 27 November 1944, 3,670 tons of stored bombs exploded, apparently detonated by the incorrect use of a brass chisel for the removal of an exploder from a bomb. Eighty-one prisoners, servicemen and civilians were killed, a huge crater still marking the site of the explosion. The blast was heard 100 miles away. What remained of the site carried on in use until 1958, storing high explosive ordnance. At a former underground quarry at Linley in Staffordshire, a reserve depot was briefly established in 1941. However quarry roof falls led to the early abandonment of the site, except for the surface storage of obsolete bombs. The lack of suitable below ground storage led to the RAF eventually operating smaller, dispersed surface dumps.

The vast quantities of explosives and ammunition being produced by the new ordnance factories led to the outstripping of the existing storage facilities both on and off the factory sites, especially with the build-up to D-Day. The factory at Swynnerton, for example, from 1940 until November 1944, filled 1,000 million rounds of small arms ammunition with explosive propellant. Temporary storage was found, such as the caves at Beech near Stone in Staffordshire and along the quiet roads between the station at Craven Arms and Brampton Bryan in Herefordshire. This latter operation was run by the Royal Army Ordnance Corps, the ammunition being stored in Nissen huts in fields or by roadsides. A more sinister depot was that used by the US Army from late 1943 for the storage of poison gas shells in hutting on Loton Deer Park at Alberbury in Shropshire; this site was equipped with an air raid siren should there be a potentially disastrous leakage of gas.

Many of the important storage facilities in the area relied on on-site locomotives *viz*: Branston, Burton-on-Trent (Ordnance Storage and Disposal Depot); Cold Meece (part of the Swynnerton complex) (Proof and Trials Unit); Donnington (COD); Honeybourne, Worcestershire (COD); Kineton, Warwickshire (CAD); Long Marston, Warwickshire (Command Engineer Park); Malvern, Worcestershire (RNAD); Moreton-on-Lugg, Herefordshire (COD); Kinnerley Junction, Shropshire (RE); Sudbury, Staffordshire (Central Vehicle Depot) and Wem (COD).

RADAR AND THE SCIENCE OF WAR 2

A.P. Rowe, the Superintendent of the Telecommunications Research Establishment, writing after the war related that, while looking out from his office at Malvern College, he had adapted the old saying and said 'this war will be won on the playing fields of Malvern'. The West Midlands' role in the development of wartime radar is arguably its finest hour and so the story will be told in some detail.

The need for early warning of the approach of enemy aircraft had been recognised during the Great War, following the initial bombing attacks on centres of population by Zeppelin airships (see chapters 8 and 9). A system was established, relying on wireless intercepts, to determine when the Germans were preparing for a raid. Sound locators of various forms were positioned on the south and east coasts to hear the approach of aircraft before they could be seen, and coast watchers and inland observers then provided information on the progress and size of the attacking force. This information was passed by telephone to the Home Defence squadrons of the Royal Flying Corps, the Royal Artillery anti-aircraft gun and searchlight sites in the predicted target areas, as well as the Chiefs of Police so that warning could be given to the civilian population of an impending attack. For the relatively slow speeds of the bombing craft of that period, this method of warning was sufficient to alert the defence

forces and, as a consequence, some enemy raids by Zeppelins were either frustrated or diverted from their main targets The Signals Experimental Establishment (SEE) of 1916 and the Searchlight Experimental Establishment (SLEE) of 1917 would in due time combine and become the Air Defence Experimental Establishment (ADEE).

2/1 The main school building of Malvern College which can be viewed from College Road in Great Malvern. This particular building was occupied by A.P. Rowe, the Superintendent, and senior staff of Telecommunications Research Establishment (TRE), as well as some of the technical and training staff from May 1942 until 1946. (Mick Wilks)

Post-war, the Army, supported by ADEE (now located at Biggin Hill in Kent), continued to look at the needs of early warning systems, basing their work primarily on the use of sound mirrors. A number of experimental concrete mirrors were built in the Romney Marsh area of Kent and on the island of Malta, the remains of which can still be seen today. The intention had been to construct a string of mirrors on the Kent and Essex coasts, but stringent military budget restrictions prevented this.

The resurgence of Germany as a military power under the Nazi regime and the consequent growth of the Luftwaffe in the early 1930s caused the Air Ministry to establish a committee under the chairmanship of Sir Henry Tizard to consider ways of dealing with the new threat of an air attack against Britain. The possibility of using 'death rays' to cripple enemy aircrew was briefly considered, but the use of radio waves to provide early warning of approaching aircraft promised a better avenue of research. Robert Watson-Watt, of the Radio Research Station at Slough, was asked by Dr Wimperis, Director of Scientific Research at the Air Ministry, to pursue the research. To test the feasibility of using radio waves in this way, Watson-Watt used the BBC's powerful transmitter at Daventry in the Midlands to provide a signal. This was reflected by an RAF Handley Page Heyford bomber over-flying the area, the reflection being picked up by a van parked on nearby Weedon Hill that contained a receiver, oscilloscope and batteries. The demonstration was conducted in February 1935, and detected the presence of an aircraft at a distance of 8 miles.

Following this successful demonstration, a small Air Ministry research station under the direction of Watson-Watt was quickly established at Orfordness on the Suffolk coast to further develop the principle of radio direction-finding. A move to Bawdsey Manor followed in May 1936, with A.P. Rowe becoming the Superintendent of the Bawdsey Research Station (BRS). It was here that the first of what were to become the Chain Home coastal radar stations was to be developed, with the capability of detecting the approach of aircraft up to a range of 100 miles. By 1937 Bawdsey had become fully operational and part of an increasing number of radar stations being established around the British coastline. In the summer of 1940 these were to be a vital element in Fighter Command's ability to counter the Luftwaffe in the Battle of Britain. It is possible that without this early warning system the battle would have been lost and, with an invasion by enemy troops following soon afterwards, the subsequent history of Britain might have been entirely different!

Alongside the Air Ministry establishment at Bawdsey, and on behalf of the Ministry of Supply, the scientists of ADEE were developing radar for use by the Army for the control of anti-aircraft and coastal defence gunnery. The Navy would also benefit from the application of this research to their warship gunnery. Meanwhile, ADEE's colleagues at Biggin Hill continued with experiments into sound mirrors and sound locators, particularly developing mobile equipment that would determine elevation and bearings of approaching aircraft. In the light of the success of radar, the work on sound mirrors for early warning purposes ended in May 1939. However, the technology of small sound locators would continue to be developed and used into the early part of the Second World War for the direction of searchlights, until the introduction of 'Elsie', a radar-controlled searchlight.

Experiments by BRS with radar equipment mounted in aircraft began in the autumn of 1936, establishing the first principles of Airborne Interception (AI) and, by the spring of 1937, aircraft-mounted equipment could also detect coastlines and shipping, leading to the development of Air to Surface Vessel (ASV) radar. At this stage, valve technology limited the radar signals to a minimum wavelength of 1½ metres, but work by a group of scientists at Birmingham University resulted in a device that could produce transmitted wavelengths of 10 centimetres. This was the cavity magnetron and it revolutionised the development of radar, giving Britain a lead over German developments. Applied to airborne radar, both AI and ASV performance improved, the latter being further developed to become the H_2S as used by Bomber Command with deadly effect to find targets at night or in poor weather. Other later electronic aids developed for Bomber Command were the navigation systems 'Gee' and 'Oboe'.

On the outbreak of war in September 1939 the research establishments left Bawdsey, the Air Ministry scientists moving to Dundee Training College to become the Air Ministry Research Establishment (AMRE), and those of ADEE moving to Christchurch in Hampshire. There they joined their colleagues from Biggin Hill, having moved there in 1938, becoming the Air Defence Research and Development Establishment (ADRDE), with Dr John Cockroft as Superintendent. A further move was made by AMRE in May 1940 to a specially prepared site at Worth Maltravers, on the Dorset coast. A year later the establishment was renamed Telecommunications Research Establishment (TRE).

In February 1942, in order to assess the radar technology that the Germans were using, British paratroops, accompanied by a radar scientist and a technician, carried out a successful raid on a German Würzburg radar site at Bruneval on the French coast. The Royal Navy were able to bring off the troops, the scientist, technician, key parts of the radar set and a number of German prisoners, these describing how the radar worked. The success of this raid highlighted the possibility of a retaliatory raid by the Germans on TRE at Worth Maltravers. Both TRE and much of ADRDE were consequently moved well inland to Malvern, in Worcestershire, where the establishments could carry on their radar development work in relative safety. The coastal defence group from ADRDE moved to Llandudno in north Wales.

Under the Government Restriction (Malvern) Order 1942, the town became a 'closed area' within which compulsory billeting was introduced to provide accommodation for the 1,000 scientists and their military support staff who now descended on the small and quiet town. A number of properties in the town had only just been

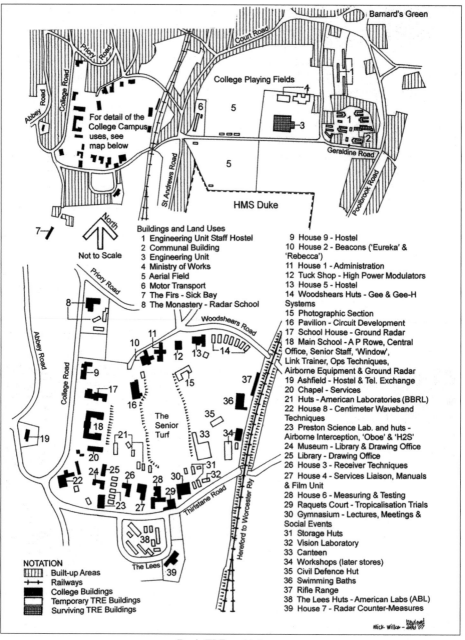

Barnard's Green

College Playing Fields

For detail of the
College Campus
uses, see
map below

Geraldine Road

HMS Duke

North

Not to Scale

Buildings and Land Uses
1 Engineering Unit Staff Hostel
2 Communal Building
3 Engineering Unit
4 Ministry of Works
5 Aerial Field
6 Motor Transport
7 The Firs - Sick Bay
8 The Monastery - Radar School

9 House 9 - Hostel
10 House 2 - Beacons ('Eureka' &
'Rebecca')
11 House 1 - Administration
12 Tuck Shop - High Power Modulators
13 House 5 - Hostel
14 Woodshears Huts - Gee & Gee-H
Systems
15 Photographic Section
16 Pavilion - Circuit Development
17 School House - Ground Radar
18 Main School - A P Rowe, Central
Office, Senior Staff, 'Window',
Link Trainer, Ops Techniques,
Airborne Equipment & Ground Radar
19 Ashfield - Hostel & Tel. Exchange
20 Chapel - Services
21 Huts - American Laboratories (BBRL)
22 House 8 - Centimeter Waveband
Techniques
23 Preston Science Lab. and huts -
Airborne Interception, 'Oboe' & 'H2S'
24 Museum - Library & Drawing Office
25 Library - Drawing Office
26 House 3 - Receiver Techniques
27 House 4 - Services Liaison, Manuals
& Film Unit
28 House 6 - Measuring & Testing
29 Raquets Court - Tropicalisation Trials
30 Gymnasium - Lectures, Meetings &
Social Events
31 Storage Huts
32 Vision Laboratory
33 Canteen
34 Workshops (later stores)
35 Civil Defence Hut
36 Swimming Baths
37 Rifle Range
38 The Lees Huts - American Labs (ABL)
39 House 7 - Radar Counter-Measures

The Senior Turf

The Lees

NOTATION
Built-up Areas
Railways
College Buildings
Temporary TRE Buildings
Surviving TRE Buildings

Mick Wilks - 2002 07

Fig 1 TRE at Malvern

14

vacated by troops of the Belgian Army and the *Cadets de la France Libre* who, in addition to British troops of the Home Defence Field Force, had occupied the town in the post-Dunkirk period, and so a 'second invasion' was not universally welcomed.

TRE at Malvern

For their scientific work, TRE occupied buildings, grounds and playing fields of Malvern Boys' College, the students and staff already having moved out once before in anticipation of the government evacuation scheme being implemented. Sleeping accommodation for TRE staff was initially in hotels, private houses and some of the College buildings, with a canteen operated by WAAFs and the WVS in the Winter Gardens. In due time, huts to accommodate stores, workshops and laboratories along with a purpose-built canteen were provided in the College

grounds, and a motor transport shed erected on part of the school playing field. The school's Preston Science Laboratory, for example, was used by Bernard Lovell (later Sir Bernard of Jodrell Bank fame) and the H_2S team, whilst one of the huts on Woodshears Road was used by staff to design the circuitry for the Bletchley Park computer. Americans working alongside both TRE and ADRDE staff, some of them since 1941, were accommodated in the County Hotel and were provided with workshops in the college grounds and on The Lees, to the south of the College. After the Americans left, the huts on The Lees were occupied by staff from the Electronics Division of the Atomic Energy Research Establishment before moving off to Harwell in 1950. Some of the hut bases there can still be seen.

By 1942, TRE had a substantial number of RAF personnel both supporting their

2/2 The Preston Science Laboratory of Malvern College, viewed from Thirlstane Road, Great Malvern. This building was occupied by the team led by Bernard Lovell (later Sir Bernard of Jodrell Bank fame), who were working on the H_2S airborne radar system, airborne interception (AI) equipment and the 'Oboe' radio navigation system from 1942. (Mick Wilks)

2/3 The Engineering Unit, off Geraldine Road, Great Malvern, was constructed for TRE in 1943, in response to a need for an expansion of production facilities for operational radar equipment. The building is now occupied by Dytecna Ltd, and continues to produce defence equipment. (Mick Wilks)

experimental work and training in the use of radar and other electronic warfare equipment. This element of the organisation was to become RAF Malvern, the headquarters staff and officers' mess being in the Abbey Hotel, whilst other ranks and WAAFs occupied the Tudor Hotel and other properties along the Wells Road. The training of both RAF personnel and scientific staff on radar equipment took place in a College building known as 'The Monastery', adjoining what was then a Roman Catholic church.

Production of radar equipment for operational use required extensive workshop facilities and in 1943 a large purpose-built permanent Engineering Unit was constructed near Geraldine Road. The building still exists. A hostel to accommodate the engineering staff was built nearby and, although most of this site has been redeveloped for housing, the communal building has been retained as part of the Chase High School. The outdoor testing of bulky electronic equipment utilised most of the remainder of the college playing fields between St Andrew's Road and Geraldine Road. (See Fig 1 for the various uses of property occupied by TRE during the Second World War.)

Close liaison between the scientists of TRE and representatives of the armed forces was maintained throughout the war by A.P. Rowe, who held a series of weekly meetings in his office known as 'Sunday Soviets' where open discussion was encouraged, ranging over operating difficulties with existing equipment and possible future research. TRE continued to occupy the College buildings until 1946, when HMS Duke vacated the TOBs off St Andrew's Road and TRE moved down the hill to occupy the site.

Guarlford Listening Station

A single hut in the middle of a field at Guarlford, a small village to the east of Malvern, is a reminder that TRE set up a radio listening post there to monitor Luftwaffe radar station radio traffic on the continent. It is said that one of the clues that there was 'something interesting' on the Baltic coast came from the recognition by one of the TRE operators at Guarlford that a particularly good German radio operator had moved there from the coast of France. Photo reconnaissance identified the rocket establishment at Peenemunde

and the consequent RAF bombing raid in August 1943 destroyed much of the facility, setting back rocket development by some months.

ADRDE in Malvern

ADRDE occupied more of the TOBs that had been built for government evacuation purposes – in this case the Home Office – on the north side of Malvern, at Pale Manor. This complex had been temporarily occupied by two Army OCTUs in 1940, then an RAF Signals School, which was still in occupation when the first ADRDE staff arrived in May 1942. Part of the site was used for accommodation of staff but the majority of the TOBs became laboratories. Other buildings were erected for ADRDE, including MT sheds, a huge engineering workshop and rather smaller specialist buildings known as 'Giraffe' and 'Lion Houses' to accommodate tall radar equipments. (See Fig 2 for the wartime uses of buildings at Pale Manor by ADRDE.) All of these buildings have recently been

2/4 This military-style hut standing in the middle of a field to the west of Guarlford, near Malvern, was a wireless listening post established by TRE for the purpose of monitoring the radio signals of Luftwaffe radar operators. It was from this building that the first clues that there was a rocket establishment at Peenemunde became apparent. (Mick Wilks)

demolished to make way for a new housing scheme.

In addition to developing radar for anti-aircraft gunnery, notably the Gun Laying Type III (GL III) that would match the American equipments for accuracy, ADRDE developed the technology to improve naval and coastal gunnery, and produced a lightweight version that would be used against flying bombs in 1944. The

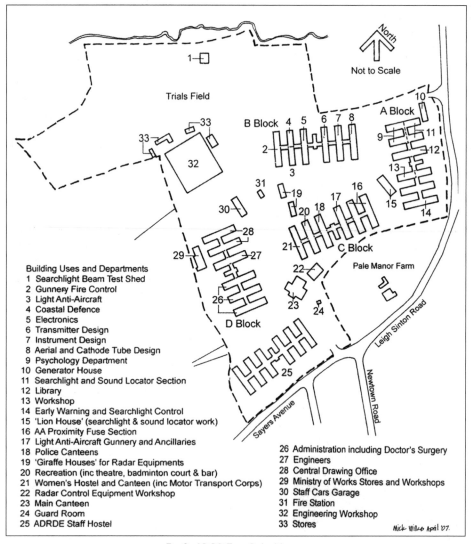

Building Uses and Departments
1 Searchlight Beam Test Shed
2 Gunnery Fire Control
3 Light Anti-Aircraft
4 Coastal Defence
5 Electronics
6 Transmitter Design
7 Instrument Design
8 Aerial and Cathode Tube Design
9 Psychology Department
10 Generator House
11 Searchlight and Sound Locator Section
12 Library
13 Workshop
14 Early Warning and Searchlight Control
15 'Lion House' (searchlight & sound locator work)
16 AA Proximity Fuse Section
17 Light Anti-Aircraft Gunnery and Ancillaries
18 Police Canteens
19 'Giraffe Houses' for Radar Equipments
20 Recreation (inc theatre, badminton court & bar)
21 Women's Hostel and Canteen (inc Motor Transport Corps)
22 Radar Control Equipment Workshop
23 Main Canteen
24 Guard Room
25 ADRDE Staff Hostel

26 Administration including Doctor's Surgery
27 Engineers
28 Central Drawing Office
29 Ministry of Works Stores and Workshops
30 Staff Cars Garage
31 Fire Station
32 Engineering Workshop
33 Stores

Mick Wilks April '07.

Fig 2 ADRDE at Pale Manor

technology was further developed to track mortar bomb trajectories and these portable battlefield versions were of enormous value in the campaign in north-west Europe when the location of enemy mortars could be quickly identified and destroyed by counter-battery fire.

ADRDE acquired a *Würzburg* radar set from Germany at the end of the war in order to assess its accuracy. The lessons learnt from it were to give the UK a post-war lead in satellite tracking and radio astronomy. The *Würzburg* was later erected near Pickersleigh Avenue in Malvern Link for use in radio astronomy, where it stood for many years and was used to track the Russian *Sputnik*. It eventually moved to Defford Airfield to continue its career in satellite tracking before being replaced by more modern equipment.

From the early days of radar in service with the British Army, ADRDE had trained REME personnel in the use of equipment. This continued at Pale Manor and on operational sites, where teams of ADRDE staff would make surprise visits to ensure that the equipment was being maintained properly and was adjusted to give optimum performance. Eventually the inspection teams were placed under the command of REME staff and out of this arrangement grew the Army Technical Services Agency (ATSA) that would be the last organisation occupying Pale Manor before its closure.

Post-war Malvern

In September 1953 the two radar research establishments in Malvern were combined to become the Radar Research Establishment (RRE), with the Pale Manor site becoming RRE North Site and the former HMS Duke site, off St Andrew's Road, RRE South Site. A Royal visit in April 1957 resulted in the establishment becoming the Royal Radar Establishment. At the same time a School of Electronics was opened at North Site to provide technical training for electronics apprentices. 1976 brought yet another name change to Royal Signals and Radar Establishment following the absorption of two signals establishments from Christchurch and Baldock. A further name change came in April 1991 to Defence Research Agency (DRA), subsequently becoming Defence Electronics Research Agency (DERA), and finally QinetiQ which now occupies the site off St Andrew's Road.

During the post-war period the establishments were involved in a wide range of electronics research including both military and civil applications of radar, air traffic control systems, missile guidance systems, infrared homing systems, laser technology, the adaptation of the wartime 'Gee' navigation system to peacetime requirements, the production of crystal semi-conductors and the development of micro-electronics.

Defford and Pershore Airfields

By 1942 TRE and ADRDE had the use of their own flying unit for carrying out experiments in connection, primarily, with the development of radar. Known by then as Telecommunications Flying Unit (TFU), it incorporated both RAF and Fleet Air Arm aircrews and ground staff, and had been formed at Christchurch Airfield. A temporary move to the larger Hurn Airfield had taken place before the move to Defford

Airfield, in Worcestershire, on the day that the scientists moved to Malvern. This airfield is located about 8 miles to the east of Malvern, near Bredon Hill. The airfield was still under construction when TFU moved in, having been created as a satellite for No 23 Operational Training Unit based at Pershore Airfield. TFU conducted their experimental flying from here until September 1957, when the introduction of fast jet aircraft and the restricted size of the airfield necessitated a move to the larger Pershore Airfield. The name of the unit was changed to Radar Research Flying Unit (RRFU) in 1955.

Despite its restricted size, Defford Airfield incorporated 67 dispersed aircraft parking pans, six having double blast pens, 23 widely dispersed blister hangars and eventually eight Type T2 hangars. Six of the latter were used for servicing TFU's own extensive collection of aircraft, the number eventually rising to over 130 aircraft of all types. Two T2s were located on the south side of the airfield where a Special Installations Unit fitted and tested H_2S radar to operational aircraft, including those of the Pathfinder Force, at a rate of eighty a year. From 1943 the USAAF would bring their Flying Fortresses for the same purpose.

At Defford, TFU, in association with TRE, was involved in the continued development of AI and ASV radars and the development of systems for improved air-to-air gunnery in poor visibility; for sensing enemy radar surveillance; for identifying the presence of enemy aircraft, and for homing-in on and jamming enemy radar stations. In addition, homing systems for RAF aircraft returning from operations, including blind approach and automatic landing, were developed. H_2S was further developed and would be adapted after the war for aerial mapping.

Although the aircraft of RRFU left Defford in 1957, some of the main runways were later used for large, track-mounted radar dishes for radio astronomy purposes, one of them being associated with the Jodrell Bank facility as a long base-line interferometer. These have now gone, but a number of 'golfballs' for satellite communication terminals occupy part of the former airfield, maintaining the electronics connection. One hangar remains close to the Defford road; a few TRE temporary brick buildings are out of sight in the woodlands but the former RAF Sick Quarters site remains in Croome Park, where part of it is being restored as a visitor centre by the National Trust.

The move to Pershore Airfield coincided with the lengthening of the main runway and provision of dispersal areas on the south side to accommodate dispersed V-bombers from Gaydon Airfield in Warwickshire. RRFU would have available a Vickers Valiant for experimental flying. The work of RRFU included research programmes for EMI, GEC and Ferranti, as well as that for the scientists at Malvern. The last task of the staff at Pershore was to convert a Buccaneer aircraft to accept the radar equipment destined for the Tornado aircraft before the station closed in December 1977.

Earls Croome Trials Unit

A unit had moved to Earls Croome from Woodyates, near Salisbury, in September

1942 to provide trials support for ADRDE at Pale Manor, it being recognised that the proving trials of various equipment would require additional support staff. No 1 Detachment of the Coastal Artillery and Anti-Aircraft Experimental Establishment (CAAEE) under the command of Major, The Lord Charnwood, came to Earls Croome in the following year. The trials field was established to the east of the village where the security gates, two huts and a Robin hangar can still be seen. A second trials ground was established to the east of Defford village, near the turning to Eckington, where security gates and fencing survive. The officers of CAAEE, a combined Royal Artillery and REME unit, and the ATS

kinetheodolite operators were billeted in the half-timbered Earls Croome Court, while the other ranks were accommodated in the outbuildings and nearby huts. The CAAEE contingent numbered almost 100 and would help in the testing of predictors and gun laying radar for Sperry and the Admiralty Gunnery Establishment (AGE) as well as ADRDE. American, Canadian and German equipment were also tested, with aircraft provided for equipment trials by the nearby TFU.

Sledge Green Radar Installation

This site was established by TRE in 1942 for testing Ground Controlled Interceptor (GCI) radar systems. Manned by RAF

2/5 This group photograph of the staff of the Coastal Artillery and Anti-Aircraft Experimental Establishment was taken outside Earl's Croome Court in Worcestershire. This combined RA and REME unit, with a large contingent of ATS, was commanded by Major The Lord Charnwood, who can be seen with the dogs in the centre of the front row. The unit provided technical support for the scientists of ADRDE at their trials ground to the east of the village. (Courtesy of the late Geoff Roberts, ex-CAAEE.)

technicians, the site was located immediately to the east of Berrow Airfield (No 5 SLG) in south Worcestershire. Most of the buildings have now gone, but an asbestos hut that was once the operations room survives as part of an agricultural holding.

AGRICULTURE 3

Despite the region containing large manufacturing complexes and urban areas agriculture was also important, with the largely rural counties of Herefordshire, Shropshire and Worcestershire contributing to the feeding of the country. The other counties also contained significant areas of farmland.

In 1915 War Agricultural Committees were set up in each county. One of their tasks was to bring into use unused land to reduce the demand for imported food, which before the war represented about 56% of home consumption. The acreage in production in 1918 was not exceeded again until 1942. Despite the increased home production there were still food shortages and rationing was introduced in 1918 but was over by 1920.

Before the outbreak of the Second World War Britain was importing over 60% of her food needs; the extra production brought about by the First World War had gradually reduced again in the inter war years due to the cheap price of imports. The advent of war and the crippling losses of shipping forced a change. Marginal land was fertilised and cultivated with machinery imported from the US and emphasis placed on the production of potatoes, sugar beet and cereal crops. By the end of the war the country was only importing 30% of her needs, albeit that food rationing had restricted these.

The civilian population was urged to 'Dig for Victory'.

To manage the vital task of improving food production, county War Agricultural Committees were again established, this time at the outbreak of war, each county having a number of district committees. These allocated machinery and foodstuffs to farms and also had draconian powers if their orders were not followed: countrywide, more than 2,000 farmers suffered dispossession. Guaranteed prices, however, made farming a more attractive proposition than pre-war. The district committees also supervised the supplementary labour brought in to carry out agricultural work (prisoners of war, Irish labour and the Women's Land Army).

In 1917 the first Women's Land Army (WLA) was founded: by 1918 it had 23,000 members. Its role was to plug the gap caused by the increasing numbers of men enlisted for war duties, and there was a pressing need to grow more food. It was therefore not too difficult to re-form the WLA in June 1939. At the start of the war it had 1,000 volunteers, many already trained, and by the end of the year its numbers had reached 4,500; by 1943 the number had soared to 80,000 women. Volunteering was replaced during the war by the direction of women into the WLA by the Ministry of Labour via Employment Exchanges.

Although a part of the Ministry of Agriculture and Fisheries, it was a quite separate organisation and was almost entirely staffed and run by women. Its Honorary Director was Lady Denman, who had played a similar role in the First World War, and it was run from her home at Balcombe Place in Sussex. From here was produced the organisation's magazine *The Land Girl*. It was Lady Denman who, with the fashion house of Worth, designed the smart, short brown overcoat worn by the women. A niggardly budget was allocated to the WLA and they were often short of uniforms; the armed forces had priority. One third of its members came from the largest cities; for example, in September 1939 46 girls from London and Lancashire were placed in Shropshire (Lancashire would provide most of Shropshire's Land Girls). Wartime experience proved that young girls from the cities could quickly adapt to their different tasks and circumstances and, after initial scepticism, they gained the confidence of the farming community. The outbreak of the war meant that male agricultural students would be in short supply, and so the country's agricultural colleges were used to train members of the WLA (a horticultural and agricultural college for

3/1 Smartly turned-out members of the Women's Land Army on the steps of Shrewsbury Technical College (now the Wakeman School). In addition to training the WLA, the college also trained RAF wireless operators in the Second World War. (Shropshire Archives & Dr Paul Stamper)

women had also been founded at Studley at the beginning of the century by the Countess of Warwick). And so the agricultural colleges, such as those at Pershore, Studley and Harper Adams College in Shropshire, were involved in training the Land Girls. This latter college had, in the First World War, trained disabled soldiers for agricultural work and also provided courses for women in farm work. However, most girls learnt 'on the job'.

The countrywide organisation of the WLA consisted of seven Regional Officers each having responsibility for a given number of counties, and each of the counties had its own office and staff, although later in the war some amalgamations took place. The County Organiser was assisted by District Representatives, the latter's role being to see to the billeting and general welfare of the Land Girls. Encounters between the different levels were not always favourable: one Land Girl in a remote part of Warwickshire got only one visit from her District Representative who, during the meeting, remained seated on her hunter! Unlike the armed forces the Land Girl was not subject to any form of discipline, the only sanction available being dismissal from the organisation. Where the employer was unsatisfactory, the local WLA representative could remove and not replace Land Girls. If this affected the performance of a farm the farmer could face stiff penalties from the local War Agricultural Committee, even removal from his own land.

The Land Girls were called upon not only to use but also to maintain the new equipment such as tractors and feed drills coming from the USA under the Lend-Lease Agreement. In addition, they dug and cleared ditches, drained marshes, thatched roofs, caught vermin, weeded, harvested, sheared and dipped sheep, milked cows and laid hedges. All this work was done during some of the coldest winters of the century, although the summers were generally good. One week's holiday a year was allowed (to be taken in the winter!), but they were also issued a restricted number of travel passes, had Sundays off, plus one complete weekend off in four.

Britain had, until the start of the war, relied on overseas imports of timber, principally from the Baltic. With the occupation of this area by Germany from 1940 only Canada could fill the gap, but convoy space was at a premium. Britain would have to make use (as far as possible) of her own resources and by the end of the war had increased production eightfold over the pre-war figure. This was still not enough for her wartime needs; any new houses would have to use one-fifth less wood in their construction and even coffins had to be made thinner! As in agriculture, women were mobilised and formed the Women's Timber Corps (its members were inevitably nicknamed 'Lumber Jills'), the organisation eventually employing 6,000 women. They carried out heavy work in the country's forests and sawmills. In these remote areas they were often badly equipped and fed, in one instance the women relying on Italian PoWs for extra rations. One unusual job performed was that of the pole selectors who were involved in a rapid census of the country's standing timber. One pair of selectors, the Misses Bellchamber and

Tuffield, were involved in pole marking and they travelled an incredible 4,000 miles around the West Midlands by train or on foot. Their vital role did not prevent the YMCA on Shrewsbury station refusing to serve them – Land Girls were not eligible for YMCA canteen privileges, unlike female members of the armed services, until August 1942; even then they were not allowed to purchase chocolate or cigarettes from YMCA canteens. They were also stopped several times and accused of being spies as they were in possession of maps. One night had to be spent in the Stafford Police 'nick' as there was no other accommodation available.

In January 1944 the organisation had 696 hostels, the majority run directly by the WLA. At this time 22,000 women were billeted in the hostels and these worked in mobile gangs, travelling from farm to farm. The requisitioned hostels ranged widely in type from castles, manor houses, old rectories, and hotels to sports pavilions, converted stables and even hen houses. Purpose-built hostels were accommodated in Ministry of Works' wooden or Nissen steel hutting, and each hostel was run by a warden. However the majority of Land Girls were billeted on farms or in nearby cottages. At September 1943 there were 32,500 women working on private farms in the country, 11,000 in horticulture, 1,600 on 'other' work, 26,300 on 'War Agricultural' duties and 4,300 in the Women's Timber Corps, a total of 75,700. By the end of 1943 there were 650 Land Girls working in Herefordshire, 1,000 in Shropshire, 777 in Staffordshire, 1,762 in Warwickshire and 1,800 in Worcestershire.

Post war rationing and the increased need to grow more food after US aid ceased in 1945 led to the continuance of the Women's Land Army until its disbandment in 1950.

The relatively brief existence of the Women's Land Army and Timber Corps, the use of often temporary accommodation and the paucity of National Archive material on the subject has meant that information on their hostels is limited. The following information though, from the The Land Girl, is intended to evoke a little of the life of the Land Girl:

Herefordshire
The county office was in St Owen Street, Hereford. The office did a brisk trade by advertising oiled wool for knitting waterproof socks in The Land Girl.

Shropshire
By August 1943, ten hostels had been established in Shropshire. One WLA volunteer

3/2 The ablutions block for the former Women's Timber Corps camp at Bishops Wood in Staffordshire. A number of now-demolished Nissen huts provided messing and sleeping accommodation. (Bernard Lowry)

in the county, Joyce Adams, wrote to *The Land Girl* to recommend the use of olive oil for protecting the skin from the effects of the sun whilst working outdoors.

Staffordshire

The first county office was at Swynnerton Rectory, replaced by a new office at 4a St Martins Place, Stafford.

At Bishops Wood was a Women's Timber Corps hostel, two of the workers being sisters who had been hairdressers before volunteering. Accommodation at the site consisted of at least three Nissen huts and an ablutions block, still surviving. Irish labour supplemented the work of these women.

Warwickshire

Ann Taylor wrote in August 1941 from a farm near Shipston-on-Stour to *The Land Girl* for a pen pal; she said that she did just about everything on the farm and had little spare time. Two girls in a Warwickshire hostel cycled 6 miles on a dark and windy night after a day's threshing to get a sprig of mistletoe for their Christmas party, whilst others queued at cake shops in Stratford-upon-Avon for party treats. This was to be the first time that the girls would be seen out of uniform.

Worcestershire

The county office was at 5 Foregate Street, Worcester. A training college is believed to have been established at Avoncroft College, Bromsgrove.

One Land Girl in Worcestershire wrote of the pleasure of picking sprouts in the snow now that she had acquired a pair of rubber gloves to wear over her issue woollen gloves. Land Girl Myatt also wrote to the *The Land Girl* of how she worked on a fruit farm, although now it was mainly given over to potatoes and corn. The fruit pickers were Jewish boys from a nearby hostel. She now appreciated the beauty of the countryside and the charm of rural life, although in the spring her job was to spray the trees with lead arsenic!

Food

To assist in the distribution of food during the Second World War emergency food stores (buffer depots) and grain silos were erected throughout the country. During the Cold War, as a nuclear attack would inevitably lead to disruption of food supplies, the system of emergency stores (buffer depots) that had been in place in the Second World War was extended. Many of the Second World War ones were re-used whilst new ones were constructed. In this region there were grain silos at Newport (Shropshire), Rugby and Stratford-upon-Avon (Warwickshire), and Hartlebury and Stourport-on-Severn (Worcestershire). The one at Hartlebury was previously used

3/3 A Second World War grain silo at Newport, Shrops. (Bernard Lowry)

3/4 A Second World War cold store in Shrewsbury. (Bernard Lowry)

by the RAF as part of No 25 MU. It still exists but has other uses now. There were cold stores at Hereford, Shrewsbury, Stourport-on-Severn, Stratford-upon-Avon, Tamworth, Warwick and Wolverhampton. Additionally there were general purpose stores at Lichfield and Uttoxeter and probably at other locations in the region. One aid to the feeding of the nation in the Second World War was the British Restaurant. The government had decided that restaurant meals would not be rationed (ie. ration coupons would not be required for such meals) and so to make such meals more widely available local authorities were allowed from 1940 onwards to open what became known as British Restaurants. (To some extent it can be argued that British Restaurants were opened so that those who did not have access to a works canteen, where meals were not rationed, could similarly get a non-rationed meal.) The equipment for them was provided by the Ministry of Food and the restaurants were opened in large halls in most towns of any size, with larger towns having more than one. Meal prices were kept low so that most people could afford them. Few of the buildings that were used still remain as most, such as the Public Hall in Worcester, have been demolished over the years.

THE WIRELESS WAR 4

The invention of wireless goes back to the late nineteenth century but it was only in the early years of the twentieth century that the transmission of sound was developed. Prior to the First World War many countries were developing long range transmissions often to communicate with their overseas territories. They were also developing wireless for military use, mainly in terms of naval communications with ships at sea. Initially, however, commercial use came before military use. At the outset of the First World War there were commercial, post office and admiralty radio stations in the UK but none of these were in the West Midlands. There is, however, evidence that at least in Worcestershire the army made experimental transmissions using mobile transmitters/receivers.

As well as commercial users, by the start of the First World War there were 2 to 3,000 amateur radio stations in the UK, but these were immediately closed down when the war started. Subsequently many of them were employed to check for illegal transmissions to the enemy.

As well as the sending and receiving of messages the First World War also saw the start of the interception of the enemy's transmissions, and this will be discussed in the second section of this chapter.

The first limited broadcasts in the UK took place in 1920 but regular broadcasting only started in 1922 and in 1926 the BBC

was given the monopoly for broadcasting. Initially there was only a transmitter in London but late in 1922 a new transmitter was installed and became operational at Witton, Birmingham. Only one programme was broadcast until a new powerful transmitter was built in 1934 at Wychbold, near Droitwich. A second programme was then broadcast from this new transmitter which emitted a powerful enough signal for the programme to be heard in most of the UK. Additionally there were Post Office transmitters at Rugby built in 1926 and used for telegrams and radio-telephone messages. During the Second World War these transmitters were used for military communications and, it is believed, were similarly used during the Falklands war. The last of the transmitters at Rugby were demolished in 2007.

The BBC started planning for war in about 1936. It was decided that at the outset of war only one programme would be broadcast and that the embryonic TV service would cease for the duration. It was agreed that the long wave transmitter at Wychbold would need to be closed down so as not to provide a navigational aid to enemy aircraft. Similarly, as it was recognised that any transmitter could provide a navigational aid, a programme was launched to erect low power transmitters throughout the country. In the event of an enemy air raid any transmitter in the area of the raid that could act as a navigational aid could be turned off. Reception for listeners, albeit of a poorer quality, would be provided from another transmitter some distance away. From 24 transmitters in 1939 the number rose to 120 by the end of the war. Among the first of the low power transmitters was the one erected in 1940 was one at Stoke-on-Trent.

Prior to the start of the Second World War the BBC broadcast a number of programmes detailing air raid precautions along with calls for volunteers for the various national services being set up. It also increased its overseas broadcasts to Europe. It recognised that London was vulnerable to bombing and planned to relocate services away from the capital. To this end it purchased Wood Norton Hall, near Evesham, and its estate in April 1939. As soon as the war started some staff were moved to Wood Norton and by 1941 almost 30% of the BBC's staff were located there. Among other locations for BBC staff were Bangor (North Wales), Bedford, Bristol and Oxford. Prior to the move to Wood Norton Hall parts of the building had been converted into studios. Early in the war Abbey Manor House on the outskirts of Evesham was requisitioned and a studio was built there too. In order to ensure that broadcasting continued even if the country was invaded buildings were requisitioned in various parts of the country where emergency studios were then created. One of these was at The Elms, Blakebrook, Kidderminster, a house since demolished. In addition to these, emergency radio stations were set up in case the BBC went off the air. In Worcester a

4/1 The transmitter station at Woofferton in Herefordshire. (Mick Wilks)

small brick building was erected near to the canal and football ground to house a small transmitter. It was planned that a local headmaster would have broadcast to the local population giving advice on what should be done if the town was about to be overrun by the enemy.

Early in the war there was the need to increase short wave broadcasts to the more distant parts of the world. To do this three new transmitter stations were built, one of which was at Woofferton, near Ludlow. These were of a special design that meant they could not be used by enemy aircraft as navigation aids. A similar system was put in place at Wychbold for medium wave broadcasts and this station was then used for broadcasts to Europe.

During the Second World War the BBC was partially under the control of the Ministry of Information and so subject to some government direction. Thus it was involved in the transmission of propaganda, as well as factual information, to occupied Europe though its overseas broadcasts. The 'V for Victory' campaign, which started in 1941, resulted in the chalking of Vs on walls throughout the occupied countries. The campaign infuriated the German occupiers who then did their own painting of Vs to obviate the campaign. Propaganda was split between 'white' and 'black' types with the latter being done by the Political Warfare Executive (see below). Basically black propaganda was not necessarily true but was designed either to mislead the enemy or to cause confusion amongst those listening. It had been agreed that the integrity of BBC broadcasts meant that they should not be involved in black propaganda. However there was a fine line between these categories and so there was much liaison between the government, the BBC and the PWE on broadcasting propaganda. Additionally the BBC broadcast coded messages to resistance workers in occupied Europe and such messages are well known from many recent BBC programmes.

The BBC was not immune to bombing; Broadcasting House in London was hit twice and the premises in Birmingham were hit once. Despite the bombing raids and turning off transmitters the national programme continued to be broadcast throughout the war. If one circuit was interrupted an alternative circuit for the dissemination of the programme to the transmitters could be used. This happened once in the West Midlands when circuits from Birmingham were put out of action through bombing and alternative circuits through Kidderminster and Wychbold were used.

4/2 The Cold War nuclear bunker at BBC, Wood Norton, in Worcestershire. (Mick Wilks)

As stated above, 'black' propaganda broadcasting was carried out by the Political Warfare Executive based in Woburn from 1941 onwards. Initially the PWE used nearby low power transmitters, but in late 1942 a high power transmitter was erected near Crowborough, East Sussex. There were no locations in the West Midlands connected with PWE.

As well as PWE, MI6 was involved in broadcasting and receiving messages from resistance bodies and spies in occupied Europe, for which it had its own radio station.

During the Cold War the BBC continued to broadcast to the USSR and Eastern Europe and was often subject to jamming. In the early years the BBC co-operated with the Voice of America to overcome the jamming by sending the same programme through a number of transmitters. (For a time in the early 1950s the Voice of America used the Woofferton transmitters.) The BBC also prepared for possible nuclear attack by building a large concrete bunker, completed in 1970, at Wood Norton (for Wood Norton's wartime history see below) to house broadcasting studios. In the event of a nuclear attack the BBC would have broadcast an immediate warning on all its services. The development of Regional Seats of Government (see chapter 9) also involved the BBC and each RSG had a BBC studio with an associated transmitter so that broadcasting could continue after the attack. The aerial of the RSG at Drakelow can still be seen and is now used as a mobile phone mast.

The aerials at both Woofferton and Wychbold are still clearly visible from nearby roads as is the aerial at Wood Norton which is on top of a nearby hill. Those staying at Wood Norton Hall, now a hotel, can see various buildings still occupied by the BBC. Abbey Manor House still exists but there is no longer a studio there; it was purpose-built and demolished a few years ago.

The 'Y' Service

The British wireless intercept organisation was developed in the First World War in order to listen to the signals flowing to and from German Zeppelins, warships and military HQs. A number of listening stations and direction finding posts were established around the coast reporting back to the Admiralty or War Office in London where decryption took place. As early as 1915 British intelligence had been able to intercept signals from Zeppelins giving warning that they were setting out to attack the British Isles. Between the wars the Foreign Office took over the control of the wartime Government Code and Cypher School, later to become Station X based at Bletchley Park; it was so named as it was the tenth of a large number of sites acquired by MI6 before the outbreak of the Second World War. Information during the war was gathered by a number of wireless intercept stations around the country, operated by the Army, Navy, RAF and Foreign Office, these being known as the 'Y' Service after the pre-war 'Y Committee'.

Intercepted German and later Japanese radio signals were passed on to Bletchley Park for decryption, if possible, the decrypted information eventually being known as *Ultra*. In addition to the wireless intercept stations listening in to enemy signals traffic, there were also a small number of Direction Finding (DF) stations around the country. These could, when requested to do so by Bletchley Park, determine by reference to a bearings from other DF stations and by using triangulation 'fix' the location and bearing from which a signal had come. Such a site was established at Perton near Wolverhampton in 1940, although no trace of this remains.

The fear of spies using radio equipment to communicate with Germany led to the establishment of the Radio Security Service, using civilian Voluntary Interceptors (VIs). These were used to search the airwaves for unauthorised signals. The success of British counter espionage, however, appears to have led to the rounding up of all enemy spies. The VIs were therefore subsequently assigned to listen into enemy continental Morse signals on set wavelengths, their completed log sheets being passed to Bletchley Park for decryption. Numbers of VIs were also drafted into the 'Y' service later in the war as there was always a shortage of operators; it is believed that in the UK over 50,000 people were employed in signals intelligence work. One VI is known to have been active in Worcester, with his equipment in a small shed and a telegraph pole in his back garden to support the aerial.

In 1939 Germany had become aware that Britain possessed radar systems similar to its own and in May the German airship *Graf Zeppelin* carried out the first electronic warfare reconnaissance flight. With an aerial array fitted under its gondola the airship flew towards East Anglia to carry out an electronic search for the British Chain Home early warning radar system. *Graf Zeppelin* transmitted position fixes back to Germany which were picked up by the new RAF intercept station at Cheadle, Staffordshire; the information was then relayed to Fighter Command, whilst at the same time British radar followed the airship's route. The German operation to detect British radar signals was a failure – apparently because they were listening for signals on the wrong wavelength – but the *Graf Zeppelin* incident had demonstrated the effectiveness of British intercept systems.

The wireless intercept control station RAF Cheadle (No 61 WU) was established at Woodhead Hall by the Air Ministry in the summer of 1938. In the Second World War it intercepted low grade, medium and high-frequency wireless traffic in Morse or plain language from German aircraft, as well as ground-to-ground tactical radio traffic. The interception of other traffic was difficult as the Luftwaffe sent most of this over landlines. RAF Cheadle's German-speaking operators became expert at identifying which bomber units had taken off from which bases, where they were assembling, and where they would rendezvous with their fighter escorts – sometimes obtaining even their height, course, speed and intended target. Luftwaffe radio operators routinely tested their radios half an hour before take off; that information alone gave early warning of the likelihood of a raid (the RAF did a similar service for the Luftwaffe equivalent, the *Horchdienst*). However, intercept intelligence lost its usefulness as the enemy adopted deception tactics such as employing decoy formations. The information was never more than a bonus and did not influence overall strategy.

RAF Cheadle became the air force's principal intercept centre, the house being extended and hutted accommodation also built. Cheadle had a wireless and teleprinter link with Hut 3 at Bletchley Park, but it was eventually able to operate semi-independently of its parent and use its own code breakers to crack low grade Luftwaffe signal codes. In addition, it built up an invaluable German air force order of battle and intercepted meteorological signals from long-range aircraft over the Atlantic, passing this on to the RAF meteorological service. By careful signals monitoring, Cheadle was able to forecast the launching of air-launched VI missiles. It was of particular importance at the time of D-Day, monitoring Luftwaffe movements, and also during the night bombing of Germany when it intercepted night fighter beacons. Often Luftwaffe signals gave sufficient information for the skilled operators to interpret without the need for code breaking. The unit continued to play an important role well into the Cold War as part of the GCHQ network.

In July 1940 the West Midlands might have played a further role in the secret war as, with the possibility of an invasion or intensive aerial bombing making the south of England unsafe, a plan was formulated for the evacuation of the Enigma and German naval sections from Bletchley Park to Peatswood Hall, near Market Drayton in Shropshire. The relo-

4/3 Woodhead Hall, Staffordshire, the site of RAF Cheadle. In the Second World War the house, and presumably other structures on the site, received a coat of ochre camouflage paint. (Bernard Lowry)

cated station would have been known as 'BQ' (Bletchley Park was referred to as 'BP'). The code breakers would have moved north in a convoy using their own cars. It is possible that only the house (now demolished) and other existing buildings would have been used, as aerial photographs taken shortly after the war show no sign of temporary hutting.

Another site involved in the 'wireless war' was The Old Rectory at Whitchurch in Shropshire. The location may have been chosen as it was by a main GPO land-line (there is a pre-war repeater station remaining on the southern outskirts of the town, now converted into use as a school) and because radio reception was good in the area. In 1940 the building had been requisitioned for use as one of the emergency HQ of III Corps. In 1941 the building was again requisitioned as a GPO Reserve Wireless Station. The building was converted and reinforced for the extra loading of people and the listening equipment for its new and secret use as a Foreign Office intercept 'Y' Station with thirty US National Radio Company receivers manned mainly by GPO female telegraph staff who would be trained in Morse code. The aerial 'farm' surrounding the rectory could pick up signals, when conditions were suitable, as far away as Japanese-occupied French Indochina. Representative routine intercepts included traffic between USSR and the USA, France and Portugal, and between Romania and Germany and Italy. Intercepted messages were, it is believed, passed to Bletchley Park in code by a Type X cipher machine located in a room in the cellar, its door

marked 'Cipher. Please knock and wait.' In 1943 a small contingent of Royal Navy personnel arrived on the site also to use the aerial array. Amongst their secret duties was listening for emergency signals from warships that, otherwise, were maintaining wireless silence.

Whitchurch 'Y' carried on into the Cold War, for example intercepting *Pravda* broadcasts and weather reports, finally closing when GCHQ moved to London and then Cheltenham in 1952.

Another important site was located at an eighteenth-century house at Newbold Revel, Warwickshire. Here was based No 370 Wireless Unit, an RAF training school for wireless intercept operators. The house remains and is now used as a Home Office training school.

The monitoring of foreign broadcasts by the Admiralty had started at the outset of the First World War from the Marconi premises in Chelmsford. In the late 1930s the BBC and the Foreign office began to monitor foreign broadcasts, the first being those in Arabic. As the situation in Europe deteriorated German and Italian broadcasts were added, and just before the start of the war a dedicated BBC Monitoring Service was established at Wood Norton near Evesham in Worcestershire. The site provided excellent radio reception and the facility would also have provided technical control should BBC Broadcasting House in London be put out of service by enemy action, with BBC Bristol taking charge of programme content. The BBC recruited a number of refugees from Europe to monitor and note foreign language broadcasts around the clock. Amongst these was the publisher, the subsequent Lord Weidenfeld, a Jewish refugee. The impact on the Evesham area of so many foreign-speaking people can only be imagined! Other people employed at Wood Norton were the poet Geoffrey Grigson and the broadcaster Gilbert Harding. One of the important products was the Daily Digest of enemy broadcasts, distributed to foreign governments in exile, the Foreign Office, Fighter Command and many others. The Service also monitored, for example, broadcasts by both sides during the invasion of the Soviet Union in 1941 to determine what was happening during the chaotic early stages. In addition to the monitoring activities a 'Y' Unit was also at Wood Norton that intercepted radio-telephone links and Home Service broadcasts from occupied countries. In 1943 the 'Y' service relocated to Caversham near Reading which, once an invasion had become unlikely, provided a more convenient location for Broadcasting House.

Evacuation to the West Midlands

Most people will be aware of the government schemes planned in the 1930s to evacuate children, pregnant women and the disabled from urban areas to the countryside as a response to the threat of enemy bombing. One of the iconic images of the Second World War is of children with their gas masks and identification labels on railway station platforms – it is regularly re-enacted in television drama documentaries. The rural areas of the West Midlands were designated as reception areas in the late 1930s and these scenes were to be enacted for real in the region from 1 September 1939, when children from Birmingham and other large cities were moved to the countryside for safety. Less well known, perhaps, are the evacuation schemes to protect the government and enable it to continue functioning under heavy bombardment.

The Rae Committee, chaired by Sir James Rae, a sub-committee of the Committee of Imperial Defence, started working on various ideas to protect the government in 1937, out of which came plans to build a number of strongly-built underground facilities in London. The Cabinet War Rooms, now open to the public, and located under the government buildings on the corner of Horse Guards Road and King Charles Street, are one manifestation of that policy. Should even these facilities have become untenable,

the plan was to move the Royal Family, the government and civil service support staff, to the relative safety of the West Midlands area. As early as 1938, and before the Munich Agreement had been signed, representatives of the Office of Works, who had an office in Worcester, were surveying the whole of the West Midlands for suitable accommodation. Worcestershire became a focus for this activity and there is good evidence that the process of requisitioning hotels, large country houses and private schools began in September 1939, with properties as far away as Bath and Birmingham also being considered.

Good communications for both government ministers and the king would have been an essential requirement in the event of their evacuation to the West Midlands if the direction and morale of the armed forces and the population as a whole was to be maintained whilst under attack. The BBC already had a presence in Worcestershire with a powerful transmitter at Wychbold, to the north of Droitwich (see chapter 4), but in 1939 a second facility was provided at Wood Norton, near Evesham. Other wireless communications, both government and military, would be located in Worcestershire, suggesting that wireless transmission and reception was particularly good here and that this, in addition to the distance from the coasts, may have

37

been a consideration in the choice of Worcestershire for the evacuation.

A two stage move was planned: government departments that had less need to be in London would be evacuated first – this was code-named 'Yellow Move' – followed by staff from the key ministries, the government, and the Royal Family – code-named 'Black Move'. The staff figures involved vary from one account to another but could have totalled as many as 90,000. The threat of an invasion of Britain, following the successes of German forces in France and Flanders and the evacuation of the BEF and French troops from Dunkirk, appears to have brought an increased sense of urgency to the evacuation scheme and some elements of Yellow Move were carried out and preparations made for the government and Royal Family to come to Worcestershire as part of Black Move. 1940 saw a number of new office developments being quickly constructed in the county known as 'Temporary Office Buildings' (TOBs) that incorporated strengthened, windowless, rooms for use as air raid shelters. These had been designed by Sir James West of the Ministry of Works in the form of twelve flat-roofed wings off a central spine and typically built in blocks of three. Many of the TOBs are still, or were until recently, occupied by government departments, but are now steadily falling to the developer's bulldozer. The precise details of the government evacuation scheme are still hazy, and few official records seem to have survived, but nevertheless a number of the elements of the move have been identified:

• Madresfield Court, near Malvern, was provisioned ready to receive the Royal Family – a move code-named 'Rocking Horse' – and a garrison of troops from the

5/1 Said to be the inspiration for the house in 'Brideshead Revisited', Madresfield Court, near Malvern, the then home of Earl Beauchamp, was made ready to receive the Royal Family as part of 'Black Move' in 1940. (Mick Wilks)

5/2 Pitchford Hall, near Shrewsbury, was also earmarked for occupation by the Royal Family. It is believed that this house would have been occupied as part of a staged withdrawal northwards, ahead of invading forces. (Bernard Lowry)

No 23 Infantry Training Centre at Norton Barracks was billeted nearby to provide a guard. A second property, Pitchford Hall in Shropshire, was also earmarked for the same purpose, suggesting that a plan for a gradual withdrawal of the Royal Family northwards and finally to Canada, possibly via Liverpool, was envisaged.

• Spetchley Court was earmarked for use by Winston Churchill. The property was subsequently used for rest and recuperation by the US Air Force.

5/3 Spetchley Court was one of many large properties earmarked for the government evacuation scheme, in this case for occupation by Winston Churchill as part of 'Black Move'. Although it was not occupied by him, the house was used later in the war by American 8th Air Force personnel for rest and recuperation. It was known to them as a 'Flak Shack'. (Mick Wilks)

5/4 The Royal Shakespeare Theatre at Stratford-upon-Avon was earmarked for full government meetings, while Cabinet meetings would have been held at Malvern College, should Black Move have occurred and ministers and their staffs have been evacuated to the Midlands.
(Bernard Lowry)

• Hindlip Hall and Bevere House, both on the north side of Worcester, were earmarked for occupation by the cabinet and their staff. Hindlip Hall was in the event occupied by No 24 Group RAF. It is now the West Mercia Police Headquarters.

• The Royal Shakespeare Theatre at Stratford-upon-Avon was apparently earmarked for full meetings of Parliament, while Malvern College was to have been the venue for Cabinet meetings.

• Malvern College was requisitioned in 1939 for occupation by the Admiralty, but then a TOB complex was built nearby in 1940 for the Admiralty. A communications facility was established initially in the Abbey Hotel, but this was later moved to a purpose-built radio station in Malvern Link. The building still exists and it was from here that the fleet would have been controlled. The Admiralty did not move to Malvern, but sent instead a basic training establishment to occupy the new buildings. This became known as HMS Duke – 'Duke' being the code name for the Admiralty evacuation scheme.

• A second complex of TOBs was built on the north side of Malvern at Pale Manor for occupation by the Ministry of Home Security. This was actually occupied by two Army OCTUs initially, then an RAF wireless training school, followed in 1942 by ADRDE (see chapter 2). The site has recently been cleared to make way for new housing.

5/5 These temporary office buildings (TOBs), now part of the University of Worcester, off Oldbury Road, St Johns, Worcester, are just a few of the many such buildings constructed in 1940 on a number of sites in Worcestershire and elsewhere for occupation by government departments evacuated from London. (Mick Wilks)

• Various buildings in Worcester, including the Kings School and Star Hotel (now Whitehouse Hotel), were temporarily occupied by officials from the Air Ministry, until TOBs in St Johns and at Whittington Road became available. Some elements of the Air Ministry occupied the new buildings for the duration of the war, and a communications facility along with a fighter control room, in readiness for Black Move, was established at the former city workhouse at Hillborough – code-named 'Longfellow'. The fighter control room was in what is now Worcester's mosque. Some of the TOBs in St Johns survive and now form part of the University of Worcester, while those at Whittington Road are, for the moment, occupied by Defra and HM Revenue & Customs.

• TOBs were constructed at Witton, Droitwich, for the War Office, and a communications facility established on a hill to the south of the town – code-named 'Chaucer'. These were occupied by various War Office departments during the war and afterwards, including the Army Veterinary Corps and most recently by the Army Medal Office.

• Bromsgrove School was earmarked for the Foreign and Commonwealth Office, and some staff from the India Office did make the move. A small number of TOBs were built on the north side of the town, presumably for the Foreign Office, but in the event were occupied by nurses at the nearby emergency hospital and at Barnsley Hall Hospital.

• Other elements of the evacuation from London included the storage of paintings from the Tate Gallery at Eastington Hall in Worcestershire and Hellens in Herefordshire (paintings were stored here temporarily before being moved firstly to Sudeley Castle and then to the Manod Quarry in Wales); the Bank of England moving to Overbury Court in South Worcestershire (a few staff were temporarily moved); the Central Clearing Bank moving to Trentham Gardens, near Stoke-on-Trent, with the Paymaster General's staff and the GPO also moving to the vicinity (for the duration of the war). Books from the Science Museum were stored temporarily at Eastington Hall and artefacts from the Natural History Museum went to How Caple Court in Herefordshire. It is interesting to note that the Birmingham Museum and Art Gallery also dispersed some of its exhibits to country houses in the region following the start of the 1940 Blitz.

The V2 rocket attacks on London in 1944 and 1945 apparently precipitated a further consideration of the Yellow and Black Moves by the government, but the launch sites on the continent were soon overrun by allied troops and the attack did not develop sufficiently to warrant any further implementation of the scheme.

ANTI INVASION DEFENCES

6

The West Midlands Region is the furthest of all of the United Kingdom regions from the sea yet, in 1940 and 1941, extensive defences were put in place to resist a possible airborne and ground attack by German forces. The successful German military campaigns in Poland, Scandinavia and then the Low Countries and France had revealed to British military planners the full panoply of the enemy's Blitzkrieg techniques, which brought them, after the fall of France, virtually to our doorstep. British troops and their commanders in the Norwegian campaign and later those of the British Expeditionary Force in France and Flanders had received first-hand battle experience with the enemy and had become aware of the Germans' use of Fifth Columnists, of subterfuge, and of parachutists to capture key positions both to sow confusion and to achieve tactical advantages in advance of conventional forces.

The rapid collapse of the Low Countries precipitated the call by the government for the recruitment of Local Defence Volunteers on 14 May 1940 (see chapter 7). Their initial task would be to check for subversive activity at traffic control points and to watch for enemy paratroopers intent on capturing key points. Armed with whatever weapons they could muster, dusk to dawn patrols and night-time observation from high land or buildings, plus the guarding of vulner-

able points was carried out by members of the LDV (soon to be known as the Home Guard). The withdrawal of the majority of the British Expeditionary Force plus French and Belgian troops from Dunkirk between 25 May and 5 June brought the possibility of a cross-channel invasion of Britain by the enemy into sharp focus.

On 27 May, General Edmund Ironside, then Chief of the General Staff, offered to take command of the Home Forces and prepare the country for defence. This offer was accepted by Winston Churchill who was present when Ironside set out his plans to a Joint Chiefs of Staff meeting on 25 June. He proposed the defence of potential landing places around the south and east coasts and the construction of a major anti-tank stop line, known as the GHQ Line, about 50 miles inland from the coast. This stop line was intended to protect London and the main industrial areas of the Midlands and the north, now involved in the emergency production of armaments and aircraft to make up for the losses of military materiel in France. The possibility of German forces occupying Ireland and undertaking a diversionary attack through Wales was also taken into account and potential landing beaches down Britain's west coast were prepared for defence. The possibility of such an attack was to have a marked influence on the layout of the defences of the West

6/1 III Corps was part of General Ironside's strategic reserve of Regular troops held inland for counter-attack purposes against attacks by enemy ground forces into the Midlands. III Corps established its headquarters in The Old Rectory at Whitchurch in Shropshire during the summer of 1940. The external buttresses seen here are from a later date, when the building was strengthened to accommodate equipment of the Y Service. (Bernard Lowry)

6/2 Evidence that Whitney Court, in west Herefordshire, was the headquarters of the 2nd London Division can still be seen in the wooded hillside beneath the court, where a number of collapsed tunnel entrances to the underground battle headquarters are apparent from the nearby public footpath. (Mick Wilks)

Midlands, containing as it did important industries (see chapter 1). It was anticipated that these would be a key objective for early capture by the enemy.

Positioned partly to the south of London but mainly in the East Midlands, Ironside gathered a strategic reserve of Regular Army troops to counter-attack the enemy once the main thrust of German ground forces had been deduced. Two divisions of that reserve were moved to the Midlands and North Wales under the control of III Corps, with their headquarters located in Whitchurch (see chapter 4), to deal with any attack from the west. In front of and behind the GHQ Line he envisaged a series of supplementary stop lines and defended nodal points around the junction of major road and rail communications in order to slow and stop enemy armoured columns (it was recognised that armoured vehicles were particularly vulnerable to attack and destruction in built-up areas). These steps were, in Ironside's words, to 'prevent them tearing the guts out of the country' as had happened in Poland and France. The fixed defences, including trench systems and pillboxes, were to be garrisoned by troops from training depots and holding camps in the area, together with men of the LDV/ Home Guard, as well as troops on airfield defence duties and on searchlight and anti-aircraft gun sites (see chapter 7). They were to buy time for the mobile columns of the strategic reserve to assemble, manoeuvre and counter-attack. A part of this force in the south-west sector of the West Midlands, plus some urban areas, would be a covert resistance organization including GHQ Auxiliary Units and Special

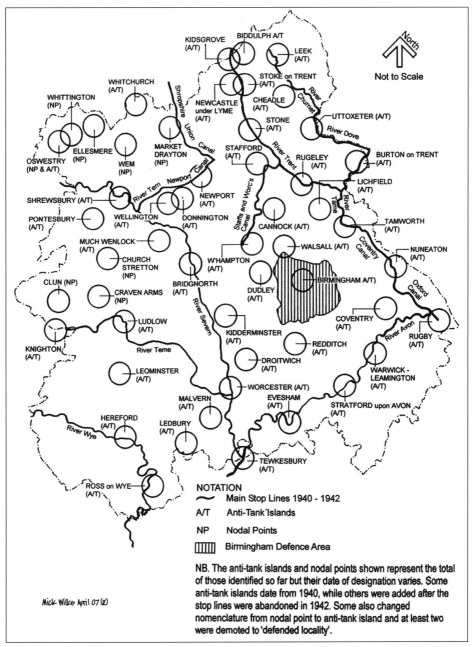

NOTATION

~ Main Stop Lines 1940 - 1942

A/T   Anti-Tank Islands

NP   Nodal Points

|||||| Birmingham Defence Area

NB. The anti-tank islands and nodal points shown represent the total of those identified so far but their date of designation varies. Some anti-tank islands date from 1940, while others were added after the stop lines were abandoned in 1942. Some also changed nomenclature from nodal point to anti-tank island and at least two were demoted to 'defended locality'.

Mick Wilkes April 07 (E)

Fig 3 West Midlands Defences 1940-1944

45

Duties Section spies; they would be called to action should any part of their area be occupied by enemy troops (see chapter 7). The first Auxiliary Units and urban resistance men and boys in the region were recruited in the late summer of 1940, with more recruited in 1941.

Ironside's broad objectives were approved by the Chiefs of Staff and Churchill and passed to the area Commands for interpretation and implementation. In the case of the West Midlands Region this was Western Command at their headquarters in Chester. Its instructions were issued to Sub-Area Commands on 5 July, proposing a series of stop lines and nodal points or anti-tank islands to be manned and prepared. Fig 3 indicates the main elements of the defences in and adjoining the West Midlands, from which it can be deduced that the main stop lines were based on ready-made anti-tank barriers formed by the main rivers and canals that, fortuitously, formed an almost complete ring around the industrial areas of Birmingham, the Black Country, Wolverhampton and Coventry. In addition the nodal points and anti-tank islands, representing the major towns and cities, sit astride the main lines of communication. These urban defences would also have protected the industries within them.

General Ironside's role as Commander in Chief of Home Forces came to an end in July 1940 when criticism of his primarily static defence methods resulted in his replacement by General Sir Alan Brooke, later Field Marshal Lord Alanbrooke, who had had the benefit of experience in the fighting in France and Flanders. Brooke advocated a more mobile form of defence, less reliant on stop lines and pillboxes. Work had stopped on such constructions by 1942 (it could not be stopped immediately due to contractual agreements) although the concept of free-standing anti-tank islands with all-round defence was retained and widened to include a hierarchy of smaller scale defended localities and centres of resistance. In many cases this involved little more than a change of name for some existing defence schemes rather than wholesale change on the ground, and so many of the features of Ironside's plan survived beyond 1940.

The task of organising the detailed siting and construction of the defences fell to the Royal Engineer Field Companies attached to III Corps, with construction manpower provided by Pioneer units, local builders and civil engineering firms, local authority manual staff, and troops of the static force, including the LDV/Home Guard. LDV/Home Guard Zone Commands also required each company or platoon commander to prepare a defence scheme for his area of responsibility, whether it be a village or factory, so that a complete web of defences would be created throughout the region, and indeed the country, through which any invading forces would have to fight. This was expected to prevent the momentum that had been achieved by enemy columns in Poland or France. The orders issued to all static forces stipulated that they should fight at their posts 'to the last man and the last round'. There was to be no withdrawal!

Communications were to form a key element of this multi-layered organization, with intelligence gathering on the invader's positions and strengths being encouraged. The LDV/Home Guard, GHQ Auxiliary Units, Special Duties spies and Observer Corps personnel would all be observing enemy activity and reporting the intelligence by message carriers, runners, motorcycle dispatch riders, civilian operated radios, telephone and carrier pigeon to military headquarters equipped with wireless transmitters, and thence to Western Command. In turn, the Area and the Sub-Area Commands would be sending back instructions and orders to the mobile counter attack columns and static troops in their areas of responsibility. All searchlight and anti-aircraft gun sites, Royal Air Force and Royal Navy units in the area had wireless transmitters that would contribute to the communications system, as would a Regular Army covert reconnaissance group code-named 'Phantom' that would operate in the vicinity of any military actions. This combined communications network was code-named 'Beetle' and was expected to avoid the problems of poor communications and intelligence that had

hampered the allies in the battle for France and Flanders.

The defences along the stop lines, around the towns and villages, around airfields and vulnerable points (such as armaments factories or munitions stores), would include road blocks, pillboxes, gun emplacements or trench systems and

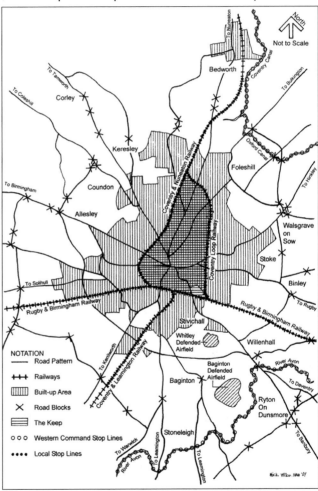

Fig 4 Coventry Anti-Tank Island Defences
September 1941

47

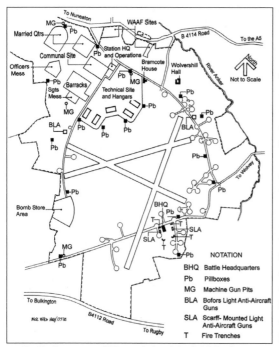

Married Qtrs

To Nuneaton

MG
Pb

WAAF Sites

B 4114 Road

To the A5

Communal Site

Station HQ
and Operations

Pb

Bramcote
House

Wolvershill
Hall

North

Not to Scale

River Anker

Officers
Mess

Pb

Barracks

Sgts
Mess

Pb

MG

Technical Site
and Hangars

Pb

Pb

Pb

MG

BLA

Pb

Pb

Pb

BLA

Pb

Pb

To Wolvey

Bomb Store
Area

Pb

BHQ
Pb

SLA

T

T

SLA

T

MG

T

Pb

Pb

Pb

NOTATION

To Bulkington

B4112 Road

Nick Wilks May '07 06

To Rugby

BHQ   Battle Headquarters
Pb   Pillboxes
MG   Machine Gun Pits
BLA   Bofors Light Anti-Aircraft
       Guns
SLA   Scarff- Mounted Light
       Anti-Aircraft Guns
T   Fire Trenches

Fig 5 Bramcote (Warwickshire) Airfield Defences

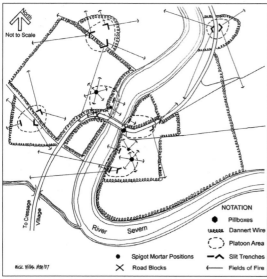

North

Not to Scale

To Cressage
Village

River   Severn

Nick Wilks Nov '07

NOTATION

●   Pillboxes
ﺴﺴﺴ   Dannert Wire
( )   Platoon Area
●   Spigot Mortar Positions   ⌐∧ Slit Trenches
✕   Road Blocks   ⟵ Fields of Fire

Fig 6 Cressage River Crossing Defences

weapons pits, barbed wire barriers or any combination of these, set out as per the instructions issued by Royal Engineer survey teams formed from the Field Companies of III Corps. The detailed location of individual defence features were carefully considered, taking into account the tactical needs of each locality, and were not as haphazardly sited as many post-war critics have thought.

Particular concern was expressed by Western Command in the summer of 1940 as to the vulnerability of the region's airfields. Not only were these vulnerable because of their offensive and defensive capabilities (the Luftwaffe attempted to destroy Fighter Command's airfields in the south of England during the Battle of Britain) but they held war reserves including aircraft, aircraft engines and other spares and material required by the RAF, and, critically, could be seized by the enemy in order to fly in troops and supplies and to fly out casualties. All airfields were therefore to be provided with defences with overhead cover (against strafing) and the approaches to them were to be protected. Eventually the Home Guard would take over the latter responsibility with the RAF Regiment being responsible for the airfield proper. The earliest structures surviving, probably dating from 1940, appear to be the large FW3/27 type pillboxes at Shawbury in Shropshire, with all round defence and a central LAA position. All new airfields up to the middle of the war, when invasion had become unlikely, were defended although no one airfield's defences were like another's, each defence scheme being worked out locally. A start on the prioritising of airfield defence assets had begun in the autumn of 1940, depending upon the position and importance of each airfield, with the release of the Taylor Report (an internal government report). In 1941, and especially after the successful but costly German airborne invasion of Crete, increased attention was paid to airfield defence with additional emphasis being put upon firepower being brought to bear on the landing area. Most of the larger defended airfields in the region from 1941 onwards were provided with new forms of defence posts, such as the Seagull Trench, together with a reinforced concrete battle headquarters from where the defence of an airfield could be co-ordinated. Fig 5 illustrates one example of an airfield defence scheme, remnants of which can still be seen from nearby roads.

A typical defence scheme for a river crossing is illustrated in Fig 6; for a small nodal point in Fig 7 and for a major anti-tank island in Fig 4; while that for a specific vulnerable point is shown in Fig 8. Similar schemes were replicated throughout the region.

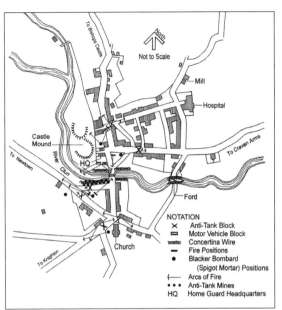

Fig 7 Clun Nodal Point Defences

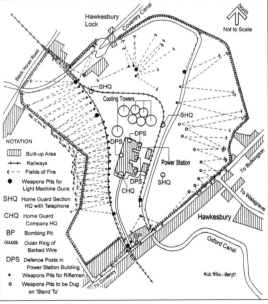

Fig 8 Hawkesbury Power Station Defences

Road Blocks

Two categories of road block were provided:

1. One of lighter construction for traffic control, where the LDV/Home Guard would draw civilian or light military traffic to a halt and check the *bona fides* of the driver and passengers to ensure that they were not enemy agents or soldiers in disguise. These blocks were generally provided in rural areas and would typically consist of scrap vehicles or farm machinery drawn partially across the road, with a barbed wire portable barrier (known as a 'knife rest' after its shape and form) being used to block temporarily the remainder of the road. This could quickly be moved to let the traffic pass after checking.

6/3 These three anti-tank cubes, and a fourth just out of sight around the corner are all that remain of a road block at the Tile Hill road junction on the west side of Coventry, and are the most substantial remnant of the Coventry Anti-Tank Island defences. This was one of a number of road blocks forming the outer of the defences indicated in Fig 4.
(Steve Carvell)

2. Heavier blocks were capable of stopping armoured vehicles, including medium tanks. These blocks would incorporate a fixed element of concrete blocks on the sides of the road to narrow down the carriageway, with a portable element that would be erected across the road just prior to an attack. This latter part of the block had to be capable of being quickly dismantled to allow counter-attack forces to use the carriageway. The portable element of the block might consist of concrete anti-tank cylinders, vertical steel rails inserted in pre-formed sockets or, for greater resistance to a charging tank, bent

Concrete Sockets

Bent Rails

4ft

4ft

The layout of a bent rail or hairpin block recommended in instructions issued in October 1940. On crossings over the Avon and Severn Stop Lines a simpler form was constructed using just one or two rows of sockets at each end of a bridge. Hairpins could also be formed by welding two lengths of rail together rather than bending as here.

Road Surface

3ft

3ft 6in — Bent Rails

Concrete Sockets

3ft 6in

12in

|← 4ft →|← 8 or 9 ft →|← 4ft →|

Section through a Bent Rail or Hairpin Block.

Fig 9 Bent Rail (or hairpin) road block

6/4 This apparently complete set of anti-tank cylinders have recently been rescued from obscurity in a nearby wood, to where they had been rolled at the end of the war from their original storage position near the road junction at Finger Post, to the west of Bewdley, in Worcestershire. The cylinders are now displayed near their original location as a result of the initiative of the local history society and sports ground committee. (Mick Wilks)

6/5 Normally used in fixed positions on soft ground alongside road blocks, or as an anti-tank barrier across open ground, 'pimples', in the form of truncated pyramids of concrete, were once numerous in the region. Those shown here can be found on the Old Leicester Road, Rugby, and have recently been moved to form a temporary vehicle barrier. (Mick Wilks)

6/6 Capable of stopping a medium tank, especially when fronted with a collection of anti-tank cylinders, the hairpin or vertical rail block was widely used in the Midlands. Heavy steel rails or RSJs (rolled steel joists) were set in sockets to form the block. When not in use, the sockets would be covered with a small concrete or iron plate, as indicated here with sockets that survive in Apley Park, north of Bridgnorth. It is likely that many other sockets survive under the post-war road surfaces in other locations. (Mick Wilks)

6/7 One of two large concrete cylinders near a canal bridge on the Oxford Canal, near Napton on the Hill, in Warwickshire. Only two were required to block a road or in this case a bridge, the cylinders being rolled into position using levers set in the holes and unlike the conventional cylinders would have been left on their side. (Mick Wilks)

6/8 Cable road blocks appear to have been popular in Worcestershire, where a steel cable would be stretched across the road to stop enemy wheeled vehicles and light tanks. This example is in a rock cutting on the road from Dunley to Heightington, and utilised two cables with a flame fougasse to form a tank trap. Two of the cable anchor points can still be seen in the rock face here as can the hollow for the 40 gallon drum of flammable liquid of the fougasse beyond. (Mick Wilks)

rails or hairpins (see Fig 9). Minefields, or a location between existing buildings or some other physical barrier, would be used to deter vehicles from circumventing the block. These heavier blocks were used on the main crossings over stop lines, in and around nodal points or anti-tank islands, or in defiles such as cuttings where, in combination with a battery of flame fougasse (see Fig 10), anti-tank grenade and sub-artillery positions, a tank trap could be formed. Road blocks of intermediate strength were sometimes used that utilised heavy steel cables stretched across the road fixed to strong anchor eyes set in rock, or steel joists set in verges, or even to substantial trees. Alternatively, large trees were earmarked for felling across a road to form such a trap. Examples of all these types of road blocks have been recorded in the West Midlands, although now only small collections of anti-tank cylinders can be found on roadsides, the occasional anchor

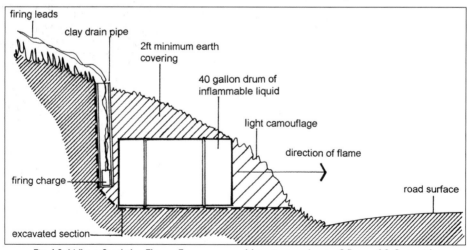

Fig 10 When fired the Flame Fougasse would project a sheet of flame 10 feet wide and 30 feet long, sufficient to disable a tank and its crew

point for cable blocks in road cuttings or steel joists in verges, and sometimes the remains of sockets in road surfaces can be seen, especially when resurfacing work is carried out.

6/11 One of several FW3/24 type pillboxes that can be seen along the River Tame Stop Line at Hopwas, near Tamworth. Fortunately, this one has been retained in the front garden of a new house, near the centre of the village, where it still overlooks Hopwas Bridge. It is six-sided but of asymmetrical form, with one long side incorporating the entrance and a pair of pistol ports. The type 24 pillbox design is the most numerous of the surviving pillboxes in the Midlands with a particularly strong representation along the stop lines in the Staffordshire area. (Mick Wilks)

6/9 This semi-sunken example of a rectangular pillbox, with additional corner loopholes, can be seen from nearby roads on the outskirts of Bramcote Airfield, Warwickshire. A number of pillboxes of this type, believed to be a local design, can still be seen in the vicinity. (Bernard Lowry)

6/12 This is one of two FW3/22 type pillboxes near the road bridge at Cressage, in Shropshire, and was part of the River Severn Stop Line defences. These pillboxes are the only tangible remains of the extensive defences around this crossing point shown in Fig 5. The equal length of all its six sides distinguish this pillbox type from the type 24 design. (Mick Wilks)

6/10 This rectangular design pillbox has been moved to Whittington Barracks, near Lichfield, where it forms part of the outdoor exhibits of the Staffordshire Regiment Museum. The pillbox once stood beside a railway line where its single pitched roof was intended to replicate a trackside hut and provide a degree of camouflage. (Mick Wilks)

6/13 Disguised as a stone built railway building, near Alton Railway Station in Staffordshire, this pillbox with the addition of a pitched roof would have provided a degree of camouflage for its occupants. The defence position formed part of the River Dove Stop Line. (Bernard Lowry)

6/14 Yet another variation on the square pillbox, this thick-walled, double-decked, shell-proof example can be seen from the lane on the south-side of the Summerfield ROF, near Kidderminster. It incorporates a light anti-aircraft gun mounting on the top and wide loopholes for automatic weapons below, and is one of five that survive on the site. (Mick Wilks)

Pillboxes

These structures of concrete or brick (with usually a concrete core) were constructed to provide protected firing positions for troops covering road blocks, for the defence of airfields, and at key factories or other vulnerable points including military stores facilities. The term pillbox appears to have been first used to describe small concrete defence positions during the Great War, when many were constructed by both the British Expeditionary Force (BEF) and the Germans along the Western Front, and others were provided along the east and south coasts of Britain for Home Defence purposes. The BEF of 1939 were to build a string of pillboxes along the Belgian border, in the anticipation that the

6/15 One of a number of the prefabricated square pillboxes that survive in the Midlands, this one can be seen alongside the Oxford Canal at Napton on the Hill, in Warwickshire. Supplied by the Stent Company, this form of pillbox would be assembled on site from internal and external concrete panels and posts bolted together, after which the space between would be filled with concrete to form a small arms-proof defence post. (Mick Wilks)

battle for France would be a repeat of that of the Great War. The failure of the allied campaign in France and Flanders against German forces, and the renewed threat of an invasion of Britain, led the War Office Directorate of Fortifications and Works to establish a branch called Fortifications and Works No 3 (FW3) that in May 1940 quickly produced drawings for a number of standard pillbox designs to accommodate the various forms of weaponry then available for use in defence schemes in Britain.

No official figures for the number of pillboxes constructed in the West Midlands have been found, but for the Western Command area (which stretched from the

6/17 An unusual variant of the rectangular pillbox are three open-topped defence positions that survive around the former Blackpole ROF. They appear to be unique to Worcester and so have been named locally as the Worcester Fortlet. This one can be viewed from a nearby footpath on the golf course at Perdiswell. (Mick Wilks)

6/16 This modern example of a pillbox can be seen close to the RAF Museum buildings at Cosford Airfield, near Wolverhampton. Called the Yarnold Sangar, after its designer, it resembles the Norcon pillbox of the Second World War and here functions as a protected guard post. (Mick Wilks)

6/18 This example of the Norcon pillbox, a variant of the type 25 round pillbox design, is essentially a large diameter concrete pipe modified to incorporate loopholes. With only four inches thickness of concrete, it would not have been proof against small arms fire without an added sandbagged surround. This one overlooks the road crossing over the River Wye at Bridge Sollers in Herefordshire, and appears to be the sole survivor of its type in the Midlands. (Mick Wilks)

Severn Estuary to the Scottish borders and included the whole of Wales, the west Midlands and north-west England) 1,589 had been completed by October 1940 and a further 776 were projected. Those that

6/19 Designed specifically for airfield defence, this low profile, mushroom-shaped, pillbox would have provided a 360 degree firing position for one or more automatic weapons. Normally constructed in groups of three, connected with zig-zag crawl trenches and located close to the perimeter track of an airfield, these structures would have formed the basis of defended localities. This one is part of a group of three that survive at Long Marston Airfield in Warwickshire. (Mick Wilks)

6/20 Another example of the low-profile airfield defence position is the 'Seagull' trench. Basically a concrete-lined trench with a concrete cover, this example can be seen at Atcham Airfield, near Shrewsbury in Shropshire. (Bernard Lowry)

remain in the West Midlands are but a very small proportion of the original number. Urban development and redevelopment has removed the majority of the fixed defences in the former nodal points and anti-tank islands, but a scatter of pillboxes can still be seen along most of the former stop lines, around many of the airfields, notably in Shropshire and Warwickshire, and at some vulnerable points. All of the main pillbox types can still be found in the region plus a number of individual designs that reflect specific tactical needs

6/21 A number of former mills along the stop lines in the region were fortified in order to provide firing points over potential river crossing points, including weirs. This is Mordiford Mill, on the River Wye Stop Line, in Herefordshire. It is currently being converted to residential use but still retains its loopholes (indicated by the projecting scaffold poles). (Mick Wilks)

at certain locations. Most pillboxes are of a thin-walled construction that would have protected the occupants from the effects of small arms fire, some have thicker shell-proof walls, whilst others are of two storeys to provide an anti-aircraft deck above the riflemen or machine-gunner's position.

Expediency and shortages of construction materials in the summer of 1940 led to the fortification of existing buildings throughout the region, notably near river crossings on the stop lines, including many of the water mills overlooking weirs. Sandbagging of existing windows to provide firing points together with the loop-holing ('mouse-holing') of walls was carried out, and a few examples of these fortified buildings can still be found in the region, as can loopholes in garden or boundary walls covering a road block or approach road to a crossing point.

Gun Emplacements

A shortage of anti-tank guns after Dunkirk led to the refurbishment and supply of 6 pdr Hotchkiss quick-firing guns that had lain in store since the First World War. Firing solid shot, in purpose-built emplacements, they would have been employed against enemy armoured vehicles, and so covered vital bridging points on the main stop lines. A number of 6 pdr emplacements were provided along the Severn and Avon Stop Lines, but just one remains now at Holt Fleet Bridge. The weapons from these positions were handed over to the Home Guard in 1941, who mounted them on locally constructed carriages to create

6/22 This emplacement appears to be the last surviving unaltered Hotchkiss 6 pdr position in the Midlands and can be found at the side of Holt Fleet Bridge, in Worcestershire. It is located on the east side of the River Severn and faces east, reflecting the function of this stop line to deal primarily with enemy attacks on the West Midlands from the west. (Mick Wilks)

mobile artillery. Later the Home Guard would also receive the Army's obsolete 2 pdr anti-tank guns.

The issue of a number of other anti-tank weapons to the Home Guard in 1941, generally classed as sub-artillery, led to the modification of many defence schemes to accommodate them. Only one of these weapons has left any meaningful archae-ology: the Spigot Mortar, also known as the Blacker Bombard. A number of the fixed concrete mountings for it have survived and can still be found, usually sited in ambush positions covering roadblocks. There is a particularly good concentration of them along the River Avon Stop Line.

Earthwork Defences

Thousands of trenches and weapons pits were dug throughout Britain to provide firing points for riflemen and machine gunners and for light anti-aircraft weapons. Such defence positions were extensively used in and around nodal points, at river crossings, on airfields and at vulner-able points. In low lying areas with high water tables, breastworks using sandbags and corrugated iron revetting would be

6/23 A number of spigot mortar emplacements survive in the region, with a particular concentration along the Avon Stop Line, in Worcestershire. However, this example can be found in the Shrewsbury Cemetery where it formed part of the anti-tank island defences covering the railway line from the south and the pre-war bypass. It is unusual in incorporating concrete 'ears' on either side of the pedestal to provide extra protection for the crew operating the weapon that would have been mounted on the stainless steel pintle. (Bernard Lowry)

6/24 Designed to accommodate a field gun, this emplacement at Lower Ellastone in Staffordshire is disguised to resemble a cattle shed, complete with corrugated iron roof supported on posts. Signs of camouflage paint can also be seen on the walls. (Bernard Lowry)

constructed to provide reasonably dry and well-drained positions. Royal Engineer instructions and drawings issued to help ensure the construction of adequate earthwork structures clearly indicate the influence of the fighting on the Western Front in the First World War! Most of the breastworks were quickly demolished and the trenches filled in to return the land to profitable use at the end of the war, but occasionally an abandoned trench can still be found in woodland areas, or a trace in pastureland where the surface of a back-filled trench has slumped. But it really requires somebody who was there at the time to identify the lumps and bumps for what they are. In some cases, though, wartime aerial photographs can be used to identify trench systems.

Barbed Wire

This material was widely used in the defences surrounding nodal points, around pillboxes and individual positions and in the construction of road blocks. Occasionally a steel picket post used to support barbed

6/25 The regional boundary in the south follows the centre of the River Severn and so the large ham (or common) seen in this aerial photograph of Tewkesbury is just outside the West Midlands regional boundary. Nevertheless, it still has a surviving grid pattern of trenches that were dug in 1940 to form aircraft landing obstacles and is perhaps the best example in the Midlands. The trenches become most apparent in times of flooding, as here. (WHEAS)

wire can be found, but most wire was collected up at the end of the war and taken into store.

Obstruction of Potential Landing Grounds

In addition to protecting airfields (see chapter 10), areas of flat open land measuring 300 yards in each direction or more were identified as offering landing grounds for enemy troop carrying aircraft, and local authorities were instructed to obstruct them by one of a number of means. Commonly, wooden or steel poles were erected at intervals over the field, or a grid pattern of trenches dug to cause damage to any aircraft attempting to land. Most of the poles have long since gone, but occasionally the trace of the grid pattern of the trenches can still be seen in meadowland. Some of the large hams alongside the River Severn, for example, still show signs of wartime trenching. Large stretches of water, both rivers and reservoirs, were also obstructed by steel cables stretched just above the water to prevent enemy float planes from safely landing.

THE HOME GUARD 7

Britain has had a long and honourable tradition of the 'weekend warrior', the volunteer and part-time soldier, and so it was natural that such a force should emerge in the dark times of two world wars.

In the First World War there existed a now almost forgotten 'Home Guard'; the Volunteer Training Corps. Born out of the fear of invasion in 1914, it was initially privately armed and its only uniform item was a 'GR' armband after the initials of the royal cipher (wags called its members 'Genuine Relics'). Only those ineligible for the forces were allowed to join. In 1915, and without any official status, the VTC were digging trenches, guarding ammunition stores etc. In 1917 the Corps became officially recognised after a new Volunteer Act replaced that of 1863 which had provided government support for locally raised volunteer defence forces. By the end of the war the Volunteers had become attached to regular army units and equipped with army uniforms. 15 battalions in all were formed in the West Midlands – one in Herefordshire, two in Shropshire, four in Staffordshire, five in Warwickshire and three in Worcestershire. Hopes that the VTC could release substantial numbers of Regular Army personnel from home defence duties proved to be illusory as the VTC lacked adequate training and equipment and with the gradual increase in the upper age for conscription it was left with only older men. It was disbanded in 1920. The next volunteer home defence force would be quite different.

The fear of the imminent fall of France in the Summer of 1940 led, on 14 May, to the Secretary of State for War, Anthony Eden, announcing on the BBC the formation of a force known as the Local Defence Volunteers. Within 24 hours of the speech a quarter of a million men had enrolled at local police stations. Two months later, at Churchill's insistence, the force was renamed the Home Guard. At its peak in 1944 it would number over 1.7m men. It was stood down on 3 December of that year. Revived in 1951, briefly and somewhat unsuccessfully during one of the Cold War crises, it was finally stood down in 1957.

Eden's primary fear expressed in his broadcast was the threat of the German parachutist and this would lead to the LDV also being known unofficially as 'Parashots'. Their role was to spot and report on enemy paratrooper landings and, if possible, to contain these. Similar concerns had occurred to Lady Helena Gleichen of Hellens, Much Marcle in Herefordshire in March 1940 when she had formed her staff and tenants into the 'Much Marcle Watchers'. It is now known that the German airborne forces' available resources for Operation Sealion would have probably consisted only of the

7/1 Officers of No 3 Home Guard Training School on the terrace of Stokesay Court in Shropshire. (By permission of Caroline Magnus)

22nd Air Landing Division and the half-formed 7 Flieger Division. This equated to one complete parachute regiment of three battalions plus the two battalions of 7 Flieger. Their allotted task – to fight as shock infantry in Operation Sealion – would have been beyond them, but their pinpoint continental operations had achieved the psychological effect of traumatising the British Government.

At best armed with a few rifles loaned by the army, or with private shotguns, homemade Molotov Cocktails to deal with enemy tanks, and little ammunition, it was a tall order for the volunteers. No uniforms were immediately available, although hurriedly printed 'LDV' or 'Home Guard' armbands were supplied. Only later in the year did significant quantities of arms from the US begin to reach the Home Guard. Apart from the 9mm Sten sub machine gun, the force would be largely dependant on US arms and US calibre ammunition. Redundant and hurriedly supplied shapeless Army denim suits would quickly be replaced by khaki woollen serge battledresses with caps bearing the proud county regiment of the wearer. On the sleeve would be worn a badge showing the county code plus the individual battalion number:

• HFD (Hereford), with 6 battalions;

• NS (North Staffordshire) and SS (South Staffordshire), with a combined total of 41 battalions;

• SHR (Shropshire, officially known as the Salop Home Guard), with 11 battalions;

• WAR (Warwickshire), with 52 battalions; and

• WOR (Worcestershire), with 12 battalions.

Once the initial invasion scare was over, and it had been adequately armed and trained (the Number 3 HG Training School was at Stokesay Court in South Shropshire), a decision had to be made as to what to do with this large force of men. Initial attempts to use the HG as part of the Field Force evaporated when it was realised that many of its members were reluctant to move away from their own areas on mobilisation; and the disruptive effect on the economy of the movement of large sections of the male workforce had to be considered. So the Home Guard gradually assumed a relatively static role, apart from its Mobile Columns. It took on responsibility for the defence of much of the country, guarding the countryside and its cities, towns and villages (themselves often turned into fortified areas known as 'centres of resistance' or 'defended localities' – see chapter 6), as well as the protection of vulnerable points (VPs) such as the approaches to airfields, and the manning of anti-aircraft batteries. The force was organized on a county basis (see above), and administered and equipped by the pre-war county Territorial Army Associations. It would emerge by the time of D-Day as a well organized and trained force, although lightly armed. Its heaviest 'conventional' ground weapons were the Hotchkiss 6 pdr and the obsolete 2 pdr AT gun that had been introduced later in the war, but was still effective against more lightly armoured vehicles. The Home Guard was, after all, not there to replace the Regular Army entirely (which still retained the primary

7/2 Members of the Broadwas Platoon of K Company of the 7th Worcestershire (Malvern) Home Guard. The photograph was taken at the company commander's house at Knightwick on the banks of the Teme. Whilst many other similar photographs exist, this is of interest as in the background is one of the now rarely found ammunition and weapon stores.
(Courtesy of Margaret Mathews)

role of the defence of the country), but would assist it by defending given localities and act as local guides and informants in the event of the Army's need.

It would be impossible to cover here the history of the Home Guard in the whole of the West Midlands. Instead of an overall summary, the organization in one of the most important areas of the region is given: Birmingham, part of the Warwickshire Home Guard. Information on individual Home Guard battalions, companies and platoons is taken from Graves' *Home Guard of Britain*, published in March 1943.

The 32 battalions of the Birmingham Home Guard formed part of the Army's Birmingham Garrison and participated in realistic exercises such as Reg 1 in the late summer of 1941. The exercise was based on the premise that the enemy had made a successful landing between Cardiff and Swansea of two infantry divisions and two Panzer regiments, and that these were advancing towards Birmingham to destroy war production facilities and strategic reserves. To make matters worse, it was deemed that there had been airborne landings in South Wales. All Regular Army troops and the Birmingham Home Guard were under the Garrison commander for the exercise, whose forces, in addition to the Home Guard, consisted of the 55th Infantry Brigade, the Czech Independent Brigade, Dutch forces, AA and Balloon Command soldiers plus members of the ROC. The principal object of the exercise was to test the military and civil defences of Birmingham and the Black Country, especially the co-operation between these

forces should the enemy attack the city. Other exercises involving the Home Guard were designed to test airfield defences, such as 'Winston' which was held in February 1942 to test those of Elmdon airfield.

May 1942 saw the introduction of the 'Stud' system (see Fig 11). The Home Guard would defend individual 'centres of resistance' in the five (later six) sectors of the city's defences. It was now more heavily armed with mines, grenades and Browning machine guns, together with unique sub-artillery consisting of the Northover Projector, the Spigot Mortar ('Blacker Bombard') and the Smith Gun. The latter two used their own special ammunition whilst the former fired the 'AW' Molotov Cocktail or the Army's standard 36M grenade. The 'AW' grenade, which contained benzene and phosphorous, was manufactured by Albright and Wilson of Oldbury. Each Sector had its own military commander who would advise on the layout of defences, and minefields were laid. Coventry's defences were meanwhile divided into two sectors. In September 1942 in the country areas outside Birmingham the defences would also be organised on a defence in depth principle, with AT islands created around the small towns and centres of resistance. Interspersed amongst these would be mobile columns of the Army and the Home Guard. Factory and fuel reserve immobilisation was also the responsibility of the Home Guard, factory and VP guarding being formalised in November 1942 with the 'Vitguard' scheme, a system for the defence of factories and other vulnerable points in response to the possi-

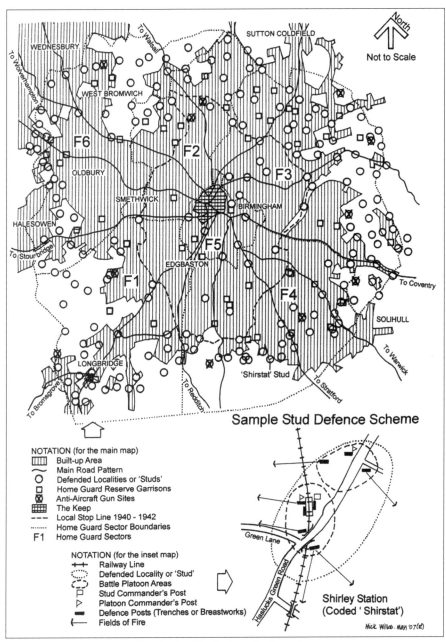

NOTATION (for the main map)
- ▥ Built-up Area
- ∿ Main Road Pattern
- ○ Defended Localities or 'Studs'
- ▢ Home Guard Reserve Garrisons
- ⊗ Anti-Aircraft Gun Sites
- ▦ The Keep
- --- Local Stop Line 1940 - 1942
- ⋯ Home Guard Sector Boundaries
- F1 Home Guard Sectors

NOTATION (for the inset map)
- ╈ Railway Line
- ⋮ Defended Locality or 'Stud'
- ⌇ Battle Platoon Areas
- ▯ Stud Commander's Post
- ▷ Platoon Commander's Post
- ▬ Defence Posts (Trenches or Breastworks)
- ← Fields of Fire

Sample Stud Defence Scheme

Shirley Station
(Coded ' Shirstat')

Nick Wilks. May '07(R)

Fig 11 The Birmingham Defence Area

65

bility of a lightning enemy paratrooper raid. The need to provide permanent guards proved immensely onerous on the Home Guard.

The 25th Warwickshire (Birmingham) Battalion included workers from a number of factories in the Aston area formed initially as static units to protect each factory. This static role was quickly forsaken for a role fighting beyond the factory boundaries. The battalion also took an early interest in street fighting training, its members being used to demonstrate such techniques (a Home Guard street fighting school was established at number 130 Bristol Street – the A38 – during the war). In 1943 the battalion became entirely mobile, trained to counter-attack. Like its Coventry brethren the battalion helped during the 1940 winter blitz, two

7/3 The former drill hall at Kington in Herefordshire, now a private house. Originally a village school, it was acquired at the beginning of the twentieth century for use by the Army Cadet Force. Before the Second World War a small bore rifle range was built at the rear of the property. In the Second World War, like the vast majority of drill halls, it was used as an HQ by the local Home Guard. (Angela Rush via Dr Mike Osborne)

of its members being killed during these operations.

On a smaller scale, the No 3 platoon of the 27th Battalion based in Selly Oak reported that in 1940 it had requisitioned four 'carbines', apparently last used by the Church Lads' Brigade forty years previously. These were used for what the Army and consequently the Home Guard quaintly referred to as 'musketry' drill before the arrival of their rifles.

The 34th Battalion was one of a number based in the Edgbaston area and they were proud to employ women auxiliaries in their signals and intelligence sections, as well as for more mundane clerical duties. This particular battalion covered the centre of the city and were equally proud to announce that they knew the area 'like a book – below ground as well as above'!

Most of those in 'B' Company of the 41st Warwickshire (Birmingham) Battalion (Edgbaston) worked in local factories, many being relatively young men in reserved occupations, although there were some First World War ex-soldiers. Most of its members had joined the LDV and had to improvise, their factories making wooden rifles for drill. The men worked long hours but attendance at Home Guard meetings was 'good'. In addition, they had to do sentry and fire watching duties during the blitz of the severe winter 1940-41, one member being awarded the MBE.

Another 'B' Company was that of 'X' Battalion, the number being omitted from Graves' wartime book for security reasons. It is possible that this was one of the BSA factory units, possibly the principal one at Small Heath? The factory had its own proof department so there was, fortunately no initial shortage of weapons and training could start straightaway. A defence scheme was drawn up, especially for those parts vital to the working of the factory, with day and night armed sentries and patrols. 'Trip barriers' were placed on the sports field as a deterrent against enemy aircraft landings. Eventually 35 defence posts were placed around the factory to guard against attacks by 'enemy parachutists, enemy transport planes and Fifth Columnists'. This factory eventually had a complement of fifteen machine guns for its defence. However, fitting it all in proved difficult for the workers: they received only one day off in seven, worked up to seventy hours per week and were consequently 'taxed to endurance'. On top of this, their place of work was a Number One Priority Factory where war production could not be prejudiced.

A rather different battalion was the 48th (Birmingham University STC), formed from members of the Senior Training Corps of Birmingham University. Its officers and instructors were drawn from the Regular Army, and its training regime was ordained and run by the War Office and not by the Home Guard. In addition, its equipment differed, it having weapons not issued to the Home Guard – e.g. the Bren light machinegun, the 2" mortar, together with 25 pdr howitzers in its artillery section. It also had field ambulances. The advantage of the force was seen to be that in the event of an emergency its undergraduate population was instantly available for mustering as part of the Home Guard. Other Birmingham

battalions were formed from LMS, City Transport and GPO employees.

Warwickshire was not, of course, wholly taken up by industry: the 4th Warwickshire (Stratford-upon-Avon) Battalion covered a large rural area, most of its members being employed in agriculture. Because of the demand for increased food production there were difficulties in the men finding time to train and drill. This was aggravated during the peak farming period of April to September, and in the severe wartime winters the men found it difficult to travel the often considerable distances from their farms to their platoon headquarters. From February 1942 it was compulsory to attend parades and train; consistent failure led to offenders being fined or even imprisoned. For men working long hours this meant that to satisfy the regulations they would be left with virtually no free time.

An important contribution was made by the Home Guard (and also the women's Auxiliary Territorial Service (ATS)) in the freeing of Regular Army men from AA Command: the 25th AA Regiment of the HG had six batteries under its control in the Birmingham area, five of these being 'Z' rocket batteries. The 26th AA Regiment contained six batteries, mainly in the Coventry area, four of these being 'Z' batteries. The Home Guard also provided LAA Troops for a number of vulnerable points such as Austin Motors at Longbridge, Humber Motors at Coventry, British Thomson-Houston at Rugby, High Duty Alloys and Reynolds Tubes at Redditch, and the Ministry of Supply Explosives Depot at Pontrilas in Herefordshire. In addition, the Home Guard provided transport columns

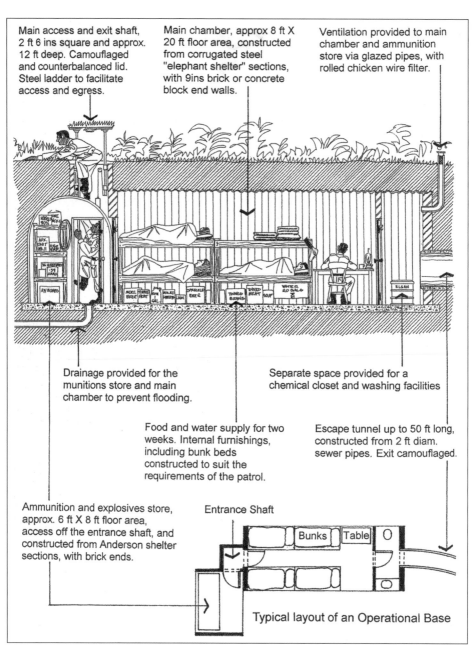

Main access and exit shaft, 2 ft 6 ins square and approx. 12 ft deep. Camouflaged and counterbalanced lid. Steel ladder to facilitate access and egress.

Main chamber, approx 8 ft X 20 ft floor area, constructed from corrugated steel "elephant shelter" sections, with 9ins brick or concrete block end walls.

Ventilation provided to main chamber and ammunition store via glazed pipes, with rolled chicken wire filter.

Drainage provided for the munitions store and main chamber to prevent flooding.

Separate space provided for a chemical closet and washing facilities

Food and water supply for two weeks. Internal furnishings, including bunk beds constructed to suit the requirements of the patrol.

Escape tunnel up to 50 ft long, constructed from 2 ft diam. sewer pipes. Exit camouflaged.

Ammunition and explosives store, approx. 6 ft X 8 ft floor area, access off the entrance shaft, and constructed from Anderson shelter sections, with brick ends.

Entrance Shaft

Bunks | Table

Typical layout of an Operational Base

Fig 12 A Worcestershire-style Auxiliary Patrol Operational Base

68

for the RASC to enable the rapid movement of large bodies of men and supplies.

This large army of men has left few tangible signs of its existence. Its meetings were held in pre-existing buildings such as drill halls and – quite often – the local pub. Small brick or corrugated steel ammunition stores were built for their use but few survive. Loopholed walls and the concrete 'thimbles' of their Spigot Mortar supports do survive together with the occasional trench system. The pillboxes of 1940 had largely fallen out of favour by the time that the Home Guard had become a viable force.

The Auxiliary Units

The fear of invasion in 1940 led to the setting up of two underground organizations: the Auxiliary Units and the Special Duties Section. The War Office, in the 1930s, had devoted research into irregular warfare and this was crystallized under the leadership of Colonel Colin Gubbins, later to head SOE. As in the southern and eastern areas of the country, a network of underground Operational Bases had been established around the coastal areas of South Wales in 1940. It is believed that an embryonic organisation was also established in Herefordshire and Worcestershire at this time, although the provision of the underground, specially built Operational Bases may not have happened until the autumn of 1940 onwards. It has been noted earlier that there was a fear of a German diversionary attack via South Wales, and it is known that there were at least fourteen Auxiliary Units patrols

of about six men each covering the main rail and road approaches from South Wales to Hereford, Worcester and the south Birmingham area. Recruited from Home Guard members in reserved occupations such as farming, its members would have literally 'gone to earth' in the event of invasion, to emerge behind the enemy's lines. Their role was to disrupt the enemy's progress by road and rail,

7/4 The interior of the 'Jehu' Auxiliary Units' patrol's underground Operational Base near Alfrick in Worcestershire in 1998. Visible here are the white painted corrugated steel panels forming the roof and walls with, at the far end, the wall containing the emergency creep exit. The photograph is taken from the entry shaft. (Bernard Lowry)

by attacking captured airfields and the enemy's headquarters, ammunition dumps, and armoured fighting vehicles. The men were uniformed and trained in unarmed combat and were heavily armed and liberally supplied with a range of explosives for their work. In addition to these groups it is believed that there were other individuals trained for assassination and in factory machinery sabotage.

Much less is known of the Special Duties Section, a network of civilian male and female spies who are believed to have also operated in the above two counties at least, and who passed intelligence information to an 'outstation' – a civilian provided with a radio who could pass information to underground Army Signal Corps 'Ground Zero Stations', such as the one still to be seen on the Blorenge near Abergavenny. Separate Intelligence Officers, generally men respected in their local areas, controlled the activities of the Auxiliary Units and Special Duties Section.

AIR DEFENCES

Following the *ad hoc* defences of the First World War, the country's defence against air attack in the next war would depend upon active means (observation, radar, anti-aircraft guns, barrage balloons, searchlights, and day and night fighter aircraft) and passive means (radio countermeasures and decoys). The West Midlands had all of these elements in place during the course of the Second World War.

The Royal Observer Corps

The Royal Observer Corps (it gained the 'Royal' citation in April 1941 after its outstanding contribution to the defeating of the German air offensive in 1940-41) had its origins in the First World War when the Metropolitan Observation Service reported on the movement of Zeppelins and bomber aircraft during attacks on the south of England. It was reactivated countrywide in the light of the expanding Luftwaffe, relying on a volunteer network of spotters who were trained to be skilled in identifying the type, number, height and direction of all aircraft flying in the vicinity of their posts, especially hostile ones. Each post (there were nearly 1,500 in the Second World War) had an elevating, plotting instrument, rotating on a gridded plan of the area of the post on a circular table. To improve the accuracy of plotting, the Micklethwaite height-correction attachment was made available at the begin-

ning of the Second World War. The posts were often little more than a sandbagged enclosure in an elevated position for the two or three observers with the minimum of weather protection. A telephone line connected each post to the Group Centre, from where information was then passed to Fighter Command, who administered the ROC.

In the event of an invasion the observers were expected to stay at their posts as long as possible reporting on enemy aircraft movements, especially troop carrying aircraft and also on the dropping of large groups of parachutists. Rifles were issued to many, if not all, of the posts. Only in the middle of the war did the Corps receive a uniform, a dark blue two-piece woollen battledress. Despite their being exposed to all weathers, no other protective clothing was issued.

Another vital wartime function performed by the ROC in the more elevated posts was code-named 'Granite'. This involved, by the use of flares, the warning of friendly aircraft should they be flying low and approaching high ground. The organization also monitored and reported on the presence of friendly aircraft that appeared to be in difficulties.

The end of the war in Europe in May 1945 saw the standing-down of the ROC that month. This was not to last as the onset of the Cold War saw the Corps

8/1 An early postwar ROC Orlit Post (right) alongside the underground monitoring post 16/B.2 at Rushton Spencer, Staffordshire. In the centre of the photograph is the entry hatch, to the left of this is the bracket for the fixed survey meter probe whilst to the far left is the air vent for the post. (Bernard Lowry)

8/2 Men of the 3/E4 post at Bromsgrove in Worcestershire stand proudly beside the entry hatch to their underground monitoring post. (The late Maurice Jones via Mick Wilks)

reactivated in January 1947. In the early 1950s the introduction of the countrywide 'Rotor' radar system led to a reorganization, for it was still felt that it had a role to play as, unlike radar, its operations could not be blocked by enemy countermeasures, even though there was increasing difficulty in plotting ever-faster and higher-flying aircraft. Countrywide, 411 posts were re-sited to better positions, whilst 93 new posts were created. To provide better protection for the observers the small, prefabricated concrete 'Orlit' post was designed. This came in two designs: 'A' rested on the ground, whilst 'B' was elevated on legs. As aircraft progressively flew ever faster and higher, the Corps continued to find it difficult to track them, especially at night, leading to a more approximate reporting system and the abandonment of the tracking instruments. From the mid-1950s its role would largely change to that of reporting on nuclear attack. It was thought that in this way it could act as a monitor of nuclear blast, providing information to civil and military authorities (in protected environments) so that they could warn and also measure the military and civil defence response.

In 1956 came the first tests of small underground monitoring posts, and eventually over 1,500 posts were constructed countrywide, together with 31 sunken or semi-sunken group headquarters. The nerve centre of the HQs, which were provided with a degree of radiation protection, was a two-storey operations room. A standard design for a small, underground or semi-underground post had emerged, of concrete, where three

8/3 The HQ of No 16 Group, ROC, in Shrewsbury. Although having lost its aerial array and other details, retains the shape of a surface ROC group HQ. It has found a new life as a veterinary practice. (Bernard Lowry)

crewmembers could work together. Two beds were provided along with rather rudimentary comforts. To perform the nuclear monitoring role instruments were mounted on the roof of the post: the fixed survey meter to measure radioactivity, the bomb power indicator to measure blast and the ground-zero indicator to measure the bearing and elevation of the blast and whether it was a ground or air burst. This information would be passed over telephone lines to the Group HQ and also to the Home Office sector control. By the early 1960s aircraft observation had virtually ceased, the ROC becoming the field force of the UK Warning and Monitoring Organisation. In addition to the ROC the UKWMO also relied upon information and warnings of attack from the various NATO radar complexes, such as RAF Fylingdales in Yorkshire. In the 1968 defence cuts 686 posts were closed, but the subsequent years saw some improvements in the comfort and equipment in the remaining posts up to the final stand down in 1992 after the fall of the Berlin Wall. Although now abandoned, many posts remain intact in the more remote parts of the West Midlands.

Anti-Aircraft Artillery

In June 1918 the anti-aircraft (AA) defences of the West Midlands had amounted to fourteen French 75 mm guns. The first three of the four Zeppelin raids on the West Midlands (see chapter 9) during the First World War were not hindered by the local fighter defences or the anti-aircraft defences; the fourth was deterred by anti-aircraft fire from approaching the centre of Birmingham. The next war would see a substantial increase in these defences.

As early as the air defence exercises of 1934, Coventry had been identified as one of the foremost key targets for enemy bombers. In 1935 there were recommendations by the Air Defence of Great Britain organisation for the strengthening of the Midlands defences: devastating enemy air raids with great loss of life were anticipated and the belief was that 'the bomber will always get through'. Despite this, by May 1937 the defences of Birmingham amounted to only two AA guns and six searchlights; by September 1940 this had grown to 64 guns in batteries, but it was still inadequate (Coventry at this time had only twenty-four guns). Just before the outbreak of war a number of mobilization depots had been built around the country to store AA guns and their equipment (several remain, such as the one opposite Tern Hill airfield). The defences relied on the mobile or static 3.7" gun, which entered production in 1937, and the less common

8/4 The late 1930s Mobilisation Depot at Elson, Ellesmere, Shropshire. The large 'up-and-over' doors allowed the storage of mobile 3.7" heavy anti-aircraft guns. (Bernard Lowry)

turreted 4.5" (there were severe delays in the production of both guns). There were also numbers of the First World War era 3" guns and small numbers of the newly introduced 40 mm Bofors light anti-aircraft gun (there was a concentration of these guns around, for example, Redditch and Rugby, the latter having eight positions). The night time location of enemy aircraft by gun and searchlight sites at the beginning of the war, before the introduction of radar, relied on sound locators but these were largely useless with the increasing speeds of aircraft. Though introduced from October 1940, the early gun laying radar sets (see chapter 2) were inaccurate and it would take time for more reliable sets to be introduced.

The responsibility for the defence of the West Midlands, amongst the other areas of Western Command, rested with the 4th AA Division of the Royal Artillery which was based at the Command HQ at

8/5 A rare surviving HAA battery position at Bannerhill near Kenilworth in Warwickshire. As battery H25 it was part of the defences of Coventry. After the war the site was retained by the MoD and as CV25 it became part of the Cold War defences of Coventry, armed with an updated version of its Second World War armament. Visible here is one of the 3.7" gun pits with ammunition lockers surrounding the gun. (Bernard Lowry)

Chester. Within the Division the 34th AA Brigade was responsible for the defence of Birmingham and Coventry and had its headquarters at 143 Birmingham Road, Sutton Coldfield. Heavy anti-aircraft protection for Coventry, for example, was provided by the 95th (Birmingham) Heavy Anti-aircraft Artillery Regiment RA (TA) with its Gun Operation Room in 1940 in Radford Road, Coventry. Gun sites at Bedworth and Binley were begun before the war and these had barracks with a cookhouse and baths. The other early war sites were at Ryton, Tile Hill, Gibbet Hill and Keresley, each battery having four static guns in protected gun pits. A protected brick and concrete command

8/6 The command post of the Bannerhill battery. Within the post were open positions for spotting binoculars, a height finder and a predictor, an early form of fire control computer. (Bernard Lowry)

8/7 The interior of one of the four gun pits of the HAA battery at The Uplands, Handsworth, Birmingham. Visible are the ready-use 3.7" ammunition lockers. (Mick Wilks)

post, provided with spotting instruments and a crude computer, controlled the operation of the guns. At the height of the blitz in January 1941 Birmingham had 100 and Coventry 40 heavy anti aircraft guns but, lacking radar, the number of aircraft brought down was small. As the war progressed the Home Guard and women's ATS took over from many of the men on the sites. The ATS were called upon to do all but load and fire the guns. The Home Guard was also responsible for a number of the 'Z' rocket batteries (see chapter 7). For the defence of strategic targets in Coventry, for example, a mobile battery of Bofors guns was provided to protect vital points such as the factories of the Standard Motors and Rootes companies; in addition to the guns surrounding the city Coventry had 56 barrage balloons directed from No 6 Balloon Centre at Wythall near Solihull, part of No 31 (Barrage Balloon) Group. Other vital sites in the West Midlands, such as Ironbridge power station and the English Abrasives factory in Stafford, relied for aerial protection on obsolete

Lewis machine guns, often also manned by the Home Guard. Although none would be as devastating as the November 1940 Coventry raid, enemy air raids would carry on into 1943 (see chapter 9).

The airfields in the region also needed protection. At the beginning of the Second World War Tern Hill, for example, had mobile, First World War vintage 3" anti-aircraft guns. New airfields were also given LAA protection; the automatic weapons provided, such as Browning or Lewis machine guns, could equally be used in a ground defence role.

Although many Second World War HAA sites were abandoned after the war it appears that at least ten sites retained their guns (usually equipped with an extra two per battery), for example those at Sutton Park, Merry Hill and Hollywood as protection against the Soviet threat. All the guns were now power operated and provided with autoloaders giving a higher rate of fire plus new gun laying radar, tied into the national Rotor radar system (see chapter 2). The batteries of the Birmingham Gun

Defended Area were controlled by 4th Group of the 74th Brigade (RA) from a reinforced concrete AA Operations Room in St Bernard's Road, Wylde Green, Birmingham (now demolished). The Coventry and Rugby GDA was controlled from the AAOR of the 4th Group of the 13th Brigade (RA) located in Stoneleigh Park of which only the 'footprint' remains. Another 28 new or existing unarmed sites

8/8 Light anti-aircraft defences on the airfield at Long Marston in Warwickshire. The design of the twin concrete positions (these seem to be formed from sewer pipes) were found on other airfields in the West Midlands. It is believed that each position held a gunner and a machine gun mounted on a pintle. (Bernard Lowry)

were identified for use by mobile 3.7" AA guns. All guns were finally removed in 1955. The West Midlands does not appear to have received the last type of AA gun, the turreted 5.25".

Barrage Balloons

These were first introduced during the First World War to defend London. The balloons formed a screen with their steel hawsers around a target – whether airfield, factory or approaches to a city – the idea being to prevent low-level attacks on the target by forcing enemy aircraft to fly higher and so reduce bombing accuracy, and also to present a better target for AA fire. RAF Balloon Command was created in 1938, with No 31 (Barrage Balloon) Group responsible for the West Midlands, the North West and Wales. A number of Balloon Centres were established. In August 1940 No 5 Balloon Centre was located at Sutton Coldfield on Rectory Road. The Centre was the parent for three balloon squadrons covering targets to the north and west of Birmingham. The balloons could be mobile and winched from the bed of a lorry or permanently tethered to steel rings set in concrete blocks. Another Balloon Centre was that mentioned above at Wythall.

Searchlights

The plan before the war was for the country to be covered by a network of searchlights. Their object was to probe for and hopefully illuminate targets for AA guns and night fighter aircraft, and to dazzle a bomber's crew. In the event a complete network was never achieved, leaving an unlit corridor which proved to be a helpful navigational aid for the Luftwaffe. To overcome this, the chief of AA Command, General Pile, ordered the concentrating of guns around the gun defended areas but this only advertised the presence of a strategic target. Selective extinguishing of searchlights from area to area and from time to time was also tried. A further but more promising change in searchlight organization at the end of 1940 saw the introduction of the more powerful 150 cm searchlight: lights would now be grouped in threes with a single powerful master light and two standard 90 cm lights. At around the same time the radar-guided searchlight, code-named 'Elsie', was also introduced. These groups were set at 10,400 yard intervals.

The third and final stage in the use of searchlights occurred in late 1941/early 1942 with the introduction of new night fighter tactics (the night fighter 'box'), the searchlights working in parallel with RAF sector operations rooms' radar control (there are slight remains of one north of Tern Hill). The searchlights were again split up, with closely spaced 'killer zones' at 6,000 yard intervals, these having priority for the 150 cm lights. The lights would be doused when a night fighter made contact with the enemy. The 90cm lights were used in the 'indicator zones' 10,400 yards apart. The fighter boxes and lights were positioned in front of the gun defended areas. The lights would also provide beacons to delineate each box, each of which covered an approximate area of 14 by 44 miles.

Most of the searchlight sites in the area quickly vanished after the war, their earth or sandbagged circular positions

8/9 A postwar view of the searchlight site at Nupend near Cradley in Herefordshire. On the right is the large earthwork protecting the later, master searchlight with, to the left of it, the more angular form of the generator's earthworks. The remains of the three earlier searchlight sites can be seen on the left; the two more intact earthworks were probably retained for a LAA position and a sound locator. Just visible in the bottom left hand corner are the corners of the hut bases of the camp. These have all now disappeared under ploughing. (WHEAS)

being razed and ploughed over if in an arable area, while the easily transportable crew hutting was removed. The ephemeral remains of the positions for the three searchlights, light AA gun, sound locator and generator have, it seems, sometimes been mistaken for Bronze Age ring ditches in the archaeological examination of aerial photographs!

Night Fighters

At the beginning of the war RAF No 12 Group was responsible for the defence of the whole of central England. In August 1940 the organization of the country's air defences was changed and the Midlands and the North West of England came under the charge of No 9 Group with its headquarters at Preston in Lancashire.

In September 1940 No 308 (Polish) Squadron was transferred to Baginton airfield near Coventry for the night fighter defence of the area; by now most enemy activity was at night but the RAF had not been prepared for this new threat. The aircraft available were standard day fighter Hurricanes and the airfield had limited facilities for the new operations. In October 1940 two sectors were created with night fighter aircraft operating from the Tern Hill and Baginton airfields, each having a sector operations room detached from the airfield. Tern Hill had Blenheim 1F night fighters, one of these being shot down in a 'friendly fire' incident in October leading to the recommendation that an IFF (Identification Friend and Foe) system should be fitted. The previous month a night fighter aircraft had shot down a Dornier Do 17 bomber. The inadequate number of fighter aircraft in the West Midlands, however, contributed to the effectiveness of the enemy's blitz.

By the end of 1940 radar-equipped aircraft began to appear but the range of their sets was very short. At the same time anti-aircraft batteries were receiving early ground laying (GL) radar sets but there was reluctance on the Army's part to pass on enemy aircraft height gleaned from radar, presumably due to some inter-service rivalry, even though this would have been useful to the night fighters.

The fighters normally patrolled on set lines above 14,000 feet in order to avoid the AA barrages but on clear nights the establishment of 'fighter nights' enabled them to operate at lower levels with the AA, by prior agreement, becoming silent. Thus on these nights the fighters switched from patrol lines to operating inside the gun defended areas. In April 1941 Boulton Paul Defiant night fighters of 96 Squadron were sent to Tern Hill in anticipation of a major raid, but technical problems and poor weather meant only three aircraft got airborne; a common frustration for the night fighter crews who would also suffer heavy losses in flying accidents.

In April 1941 a ground controlled intercept radar station was opened at Hack Green just inside the Cheshire border, covering the approaches to the Tern Hill Sector with the Comberton station (actually near the village of Wick) in Worcestershire covering the southern sector (see chapter 2). RAF Comberton was the only operational GCI radar station established in the West Midlands and was one of five inland radar stations activated in the spring of 1941 as a response to the night blitz by the Luftwaffe. The first equipment to arrive was of an 'Intermediate Transportable Type', the information from which would be fed to a separate plotting room from where night-fighter controlling would be conducted. In May 1943 RAF Comberton was upgraded to a 'Final GCI Station' with Type 7 Radar, capable of multiple aircraft controlling, long range and better height finding capabilities. A brick-built operations room, known as the 'Happidrome', and a number of ancillary rooms were erected on the site at this time. The site was uprated again during the Cold War period as part of the 'Rotor' system and an additional above ground concrete operations room was built with eight aerial plinths. The site seems to have been abandoned soon afterwards and now forms part of Glenmore Farm. While most of the buildings have now gone, the wartime Happidrome survives along with some of the radar plinths. Initially the RAF and WAAF crew were accommodated in the village of Wick, and one temporary brick and asbestos hut can be glimpsed behind Vandyke Court, but later a purpose-built camp was provided at Pinvin, to the north of Pershore, where only a Braithewaite water tower remains on what is now an industrial estate.

The following month saw the introduction of 'fighter boxes', the area being delineated by clusters of flares 30 miles apart, the night fighters forming 'queues', with twin-engined aircraft such as the soon to be introduced Bristol Beaufighter covering the approaches, and single-engined aircraft covering the actual target area. By the middle of the year the strength of No 9 Group had reached 39 aircraft, the majority being Defiants. That month a Beaufighter from High Ercall airfield, guided by the Comberton ground controlled interception station (GCI) destroyed a Heinkel III.

At the end of the year the two sectors were covered from the airfields at Honiley in Warwickshire and Atcham in Shropshire. The beginning of 1942 saw the introduction of radar into the all-black Defiants. The last wartime night fighter, the de Havilland Mosquito, appeared at Honiley in March 1943 but eighteen months later the lack of enemy activity led to the disbandment of No 9 Group. Thirty-six enemy aircraft had been destroyed by its aircraft during its active life.

Radio countermeasures

The detection in June 1940 of a suspected Luftwaffe navigation beam by RAF Cheadle led to the establishment of No 80 (Signals) Wing at Radlett in Hertfordshire the same month. One of the first priorities was the setting up of masking beacons ('Meacons') to jam the *Knickebein* (literally 'crooked leg') navigation beams by re-radiating the signals back towards the continental transmitters. These early jamming systems were given the code-name 'Aspirin'. The two Luftwaffe transmitters for targets in the Midlands were located at Calais and at Cherbourg. Enemy pathfinder aircraft followed one of the beams and at the point where the beams crossed (the target) marker flares were dropped. In August 1940 occurred the detection of a new signal, named *X-Gerät* (code-named by the RAF 'Ruffian', the countermeasures were 'Bromide').

These early radio countermeasures operations used transmitter machinery from Army or Naval stocks. Four stations were located in the West Midlands: at Hagley on Clent Hill (this later becoming a headquarters, responsible for the running of the other outstations), Kenilworth, Cookhill (known as RAF Alcester) and Mow Cop, with another just out of the area at Birdlip, Gloucestershire, and covering the southern approaches to the Midlands.

Perhaps the most controversial use of these countermeasures occurred at the time of the devastating bombing attack on Coventry on the night of the 14 November 1940, code-named by the Luftwaffe 'Moonlight Sonata'. British intelligence had become aware through Bletchley Park of the preparation of a major Luftwaffe attack on one of three Midlands targets (Coventry, Wolverhampton or Birmingham) during the period of a full moon. Enemy navigational beams were detected on 14 November, the 'Meacons' were activated, but it appears these did not have the required setting to jam the beams. In the event, the Luftwaffe navigators of the pathfinder group *Kampfgruppe (KG) 100* had little difficulty, given the bright moonlit conditions, in identifying their target and accurately dropping their marker flares. The following bombers bombed on the flares with devastating results. Of the 509 bombers that left their bases in France following the navigators of *KG100*, 449 reached their target. Only two aircraft were claimed to have been shot down by Midlands HAA batteries: one aircraft by a battery at Loughborough and one by a Birmingham battery. Although the RAF

mounted over 100 fighter sorties against the aerial armada none were shot down. A further major raid five weeks later on Birmingham saw the 'meacons' correctly set and activated. This raid turned out to be a failure, foiled as much by bad weather as by the countermeasures.

The final Luftwaffe navigation system, *Y-Gerät*, was introduced in November 1940; this was a single beam (code-named by the British 'Benito', the jammers code-named 'Benjamin'). It was more accurate, but was not fully operational until early 1941 and by then jamming was able to largely defeat the beams.

The operations of No 80 Wing became increasingly sophisticated as the war progressed. When the wireless interceptors at RAF Cheadle detected the signals used to signal the activation of the Luftwaffe navigational beacons, 'Meacon Control' at Radlett was alerted; they in turn alerted the jamming stations. Local decoy controls were alerted by 'Starfish Control' and fed information as the raid developed. In addition, Bletchley Park could often, from breaking codes, determine the bombers' target and alert No 80 Wing. This information would be passed in a guarded fashion to the different control rooms at the target. This could lead to the fire services extinguishing flares and incendiaries so that decoy 'Starfish' sites could be activated. If codes had not been broken, the 'Y' outstations could seek out the beams, whether approach or cross beams, and then the jammers would be alerted. It is unclear if any of the buildings used by the jamming stations have survived: they appear to have consisted only of a wooden hut with sandbag blast protection. Telephone and power lines were led to the hut and a generator for reserve power was on site. Loop aerials for the transmitter and direction-finding were mounted on the roof of the hut.

Bombing Decoys

Early experiments with decoys began just after the outbreak of war in November 1939, and consisted of decoy airfields close to the parent airfield and equipped with dummy aircraft and buildings (K sites). They proved to be ineffective and wasteful in land and were quickly abandoned. Although there were no official dummy airfields in the West Midlands it is known that in September 1940 dummy aircraft were scattered around the fields close to Tern Hill airfield. In addition there were two decoy factories for the Boulton Paul (Wolverhampton) and Armstrong Whitworth (Baginton) aircraft factories. Dummy buildings were erected a few miles from the actual sites. These too were quickly abandoned and replaced by night bombing decoys (see below). The Luftwaffe's night bombing offensive in the winter of 1940 meant a change of tactics and fire decoys ('SF' or 'Special Fires', also known as 'Starfish') began to be built from November 1940. These relied on a range of fire effects to lure Luftwaffe bombers to bomb on the fires and not on the actual target.

From the summer of 1941 two new types of decoy emerged, the 'QL' and 'QF', often combined on the same site. The 'Q' indicated a decoy, the 'L' a lighting effect decoy and the 'F' a fire effect. The 'QL'

sought to replicate the appearance of lights on a particular target under blackout conditions where some permitted light might be seen; for example at a factory where light might escape from an opened door, or at a railway marshalling yard where there might be dim overhead lighting or locomotive firebox glow. A particular example of this latter type of decoy was the 'QL' site at Barby for the important Rugby marshalling yard. A 'QF' site would provide the desired fire effects. Major airfields had a 'Q' site, sometimes with 'QF' effects; such sites represented the appearance of an airfield's landing lights which would be dimmed or extinguished at the enemy's approach to give verisimilitude. The small protected brick and concrete bunkers (which might also contain one or more generators for the lighting effects) from which Army, Navy and RAF crews operated the decoys, often survive.

8/10 The control bunker for the QL/QF decoy at Shutlanehead near Keele in Staffordshire. This particular decoy protected the large coal mine at Wolstanton near Newcastle-under-Lyme, Staffordshire. On the far right is the blast wall that protected the entrance whilst on the roof is an observation/escape hatch. Soil would originally have been mounded against its walls to give extra protection. (Bernard Lowry)

CIVIL DEFENCE

Air Raid Precautions

The development of the aeroplane in the twentieth century led to the air raid becoming an instrument of war. The First World War saw the first air raids on the United Kingdom with the first attempt (on Dover) in December 1914. Early in the First World War the bomb carrying capacity of aircraft was small and their range limited so that the first serious air raids on Britain were carried out by airships (Zeppelins). Even by the end of that war the range of the then aircraft was not sufficient to reach the West Midlands but this was to change by the start of the Second World War.

The first air raid to hit the West Midlands occurred on the night of 31 January/1 February 1916. Two Zeppelins bombed Burton-on-Trent, Stoke-on-Trent, Dudley, Tipton, Bradley, Wednesbury and Walsall. They were part of a much larger raid in which a total of 71 persons were killed (48 in the West Midlands) and many more injured. There were three further raids on the West Midlands by Zeppelins – one each in 1916, 1917 and 1918. The earlier one was on The Potteries and the other two on the Birmingham/Coventry area. There were no casualties from these raids but some damage; the 1917 one caused minor damage at Longbridge.

During the First World War air raid precautions were the responsibility of local councils and they were empowered to use lighting restrictions (i.e. blackout) when an air raid was imminent. The major problem here was to know when a raid would happen. Some areas bombed in the 1916 raid were not covered by lighting restrictions and this resulted in an extension of these restrictions to all of the West Midlands except Herefordshire. Also in 1916 a national warning system was introduced so that prior information of a raid could be passed to local authorities to enable them to warn the public. Various methods were used to convey the warnings, including bells and hooters. As public shelters were not provided during the First World War the public, on hearing the warning, were left to seek shelter in cellars or under railway arches, or to head for the open countryside. Clamour for public shelters increased during 1917 and some action to use buildings for this purpose was undertaken by the government, but this mainly related to London, which bore the brunt of bombing in 1917 and 1918.

After the end of the First World War consideration of the effects of bombing continued and led the government in 1924 to set up an Air Raid Precautions (ARP) Committee. This issued several reports and in 1935 an ARP Department was set up in the Home Office. The first circular on ARP was sent by the Home Office to all local authorities in that same year. In 1937 the air raid warden service was established and an Act of Parliament was passed putting the responsibility for ARP on local authorities. The Act came into force on 1 January 1938 and set out what the local authorities were to put in place. These included shelters for the public, dealing with casualties, bomb damage and fire services. Also in 1938 a plan for the appointment of regional commissioners was drawn up, and it was made public in 1939. The commissioners were to be responsible for co-ordinating civil defence within their region (they would have a wider role if an invasion took place). The West Midlands was No 9 Region and Lord Dudley was appointed commissioner based in Birmingham. A further Act – the Civil Defence Act – was passed in 1939 which gave the government more powers and put the ARP service on a statutory basis.

In 1938, at the time of the Munich crisis, many trenches were dug in public parks to act as public air raid shelters. Later some of these were made more permanent by lining and covering them. After the Munich crisis the government

9/2 Surface air raid shelter at Croome Park, Worcestershire (originally part of RAF Defford). (Colin Jones)

9/3 Warning sign from a surface shelter. (WHEAS)

began looking at the provision of domestic shelters for individual households. As a result, in 1939 production started of the Anderson shelter, named after Sir John Anderson, who was Lord Privy Seal at the time and had become responsible for the ARP Department within the Home Office. These were formed from corrugated iron sections that could be easily erected in back gardens. They were to be semi-sunk in the ground with the soil that was excavated laid over the top. The shelters were to be free to all households with income of less than £250 per year and over two and a half million were issued.

It was soon realised that these were not suitable for all circumstances and local

9/1 Reconstructed Anderson Shelter at the Regimental Museum at Whittington Barracks, Staffordshire. (Mick Wilks)

authorities were authorized to construct brick and concrete surface shelters for public use. Some of these were built on waste land but many were built on roads and streets. Others were built in school playgrounds and in factory yards. Many thousands were built throughout the country, of varying sizes but to a common design. In urban areas subject to frequent bombing many such shelters of this type were either built as or turned into dormitory shelters where the public could spend the night. Another type of shelter was the Stanton, a large semi-sunken shelter constructed from pre-cast concrete sections which were produced by the Stanton Company. These shelters were constructed on sites of military or civil importance so that the workers could shelter when a raid was taking place. In addition to these, many companies and members of the public constructed shelters to their own design, some of which still remain.

Because bombing could occur at any time of the day or night it was also necessary to provide shelters for shoppers in

9/4 Stanton air raid shelter, Sutton Road, near Market Drayton, Shropshire.
(Bernard Lowry)

9/5 Interior of a Stanton shelter.
(Colin Jones)

town centres and this was often achieved by strengthening basements of shops. In some cases strengthening of house basements was also done rather than providing Anderson shelters. The last development of a shelter took place in 1941 – an indoor shelter known as the Morrison after the then Home Secretary. This was essentially a large metal container with mesh sides that would fit under the dining room table. These continued to be manufactured and issued up to 1944.

To give warning of air raids a large organisation had been put in place. As stated earlier a network of air raid wardens had been created reporting to control centres – often the local town hall or police station. The location of the air raid warden's post was known to all those in his or her area and there was a sign outside identifying it. Air raid warning sirens were placed on tall buildings and when these sounded the alarm the wardens were responsible for getting the public into the shelters. After the air raid was over they reported on the damage in their area and advised what services were required. They were also responsible for enforcing the blackout.

Under the legislation setting up the civil defence services local authorities had to deal with casualties. To do this first aid parties were set up, often from Red Cross and St John Ambulance personnel, to render medical assistance at the site of the bombing. First aid posts were set up, continuously manned by a doctor and nurses, to treat casualties who needed a doctor but did not require hospitalization. In addition, first aid points were set up where bandages, medicines and other equipment was stored. First aid posts would often be based at a local clinic or surgery whereas first aid points would be located in a convenient building, often a village or parish hall. At the same time rescue parties were established to recover casualties from bombed buildings. These were usually local building firms who would also be called on to shore up unsound buildings or to demolish them if there was no alternative.

As well as bombs, the government feared that poison gas might be dropped. This fear was based on the experiences of poison gas in the trenches in the First World War. Design of a gas mask commenced in 1935 and by the end of 1936 was in production; it was planned to have 40 million available by the summer of 1938. Distribution of gas masks commenced at the time of the Munich crisis and had been more or less completed by the start of the Second World War. By the time distribution finally ended some 44 million had been issued.

Because of the threat of gas attacks local authorities had to arrange for decon-tamination centres where people could shower and get clean clothes. Often swimming pools were so designated as they had shower facilities, as were factories with such provision. In a few cases shower blocks were provided in or added to existing buildings. In the event there were no gas attacks and these preparations proved unnecessary.

Local authorities were also responsible for what can be called post-raid services. Of top priority was the provision of rest centres for those made homeless by the bombing. Schools in larger towns were often nominated for these purposes as they had large halls and kitchens. In other cases clubs and larger premises such as church halls were requisitioned. The rest centres were usually staffed by the WVS, which had been set up in 1938 to encourage women to assist in ARP work (in 1966 the WVS became the WRVS). For people whose homes had been destroyed or damaged beyond use, rest centres were the place where they would be helped to find alternative accommodation and given financial assistance.

The industrial parts of the West Midlands were heavily bombed during the Second World War, particularly in 1940 and 1941. The most infamous raid was the one on Coventry in November 1940. Birmingham was bombed over 50 times with raids continuing till 1943. Bombs caused the deaths of over a thousand people in Coventry, and over two thousand in Birmingham, as well as many in the other industrial centres in the Black Country and The Potteries. Other towns and villages in the West Midlands suffered from bombing raids either as targets or because the bombers had misread their position or jettisoned their bombs prior to returning home. Other bombs were dropped on decoy sites (see chapter 8) which, of course, was the purpose of such sites. Exceptionally, Shropshire even received one flying bomb (V1) in December 1944 which landed near Newport damaging some property. Apparently it had been launched from an enemy aircraft and had been aimed at Manchester.

The ARP services put in place were invaluable in giving warnings prior to raids and clearing up afterwards. Most of this ARP work took place in existing buildings, many of which remain. In isolated cases the indication of an air raid warden's post can still be seen, but in most cases one would never know the connection of a building with ARP duties. Some brick and concrete shelters remain, usually turned into a storage building; this is often the case at schools. However most went soon after the war as they were partially blocking roads. It is still possible to see Stanton shelters but usually they are on sites inaccessible to the general public. The only Anderson shelters the authors have seen, other than in photographs, have been dug out and re-erected as garden sheds. The sections of Anderson shelters were also used by the Home Guard to build ammunition stores and the remains of these can sometimes be seen (see chapter 7). Finally, it is sometimes possible to see an air raid warning siren remaining on a tall building, but even these are now few and far between.

Cold War

With the start of the Cold War in the late 1940s civil defence again became an issue. A new Civil Defence Act was passed in 1948 and in 1949 a Civil Defence Corps was set up which was to have much the same responsibilities as in the Second World War. Responsibility for organization, recruitment and training was placed on County Councils. Whilst there were national training schools there were also training centres in each county. In Staffordshire the training centre was at Swynnerton and in Worcestershire at Hampton Lovett. The Civil Defence Corps was disbanded in 1969 and the training schools were closed. From then until the end of the Cold War civil defence planning continued within government circles only. Whilst on several occasions discussions had taken place on shelters to protect the public from nuclear fallout, none were ever constructed by the government although some members of the public constructed their own. However the government did construct underground bunkers for its own services (on which see below).

In the event of a nuclear attack communications would be vital. The immediate post-war telephone system was susceptible to disruption caused by bombing as was seen during the Second World War. Initially in the Cold War emergency telephone exchanges were constructed underground in hardened bunkers to obviate the risks of bombing. One of these was the Anchor Exchange in Birmingham. Apparently the bunkers still remain but are mainly inaccessible because of safety problems. In addition to underground exchanges a number of protected telephone repeater stations were built, including one in Birmingham and one in Sandwell. The development of microwave systems enabled a more secure communications network to be introduced in the 1950s (known as 'Backbone') with transmission masts being erected throughout the country. Parts of this network were the Post Office (now BT) Tower in Birmingham and the microwave tower at Pye Green on Cannock Chase. In addition to this system

9/6 Microwave Tower, Pye Green, Cannock, Staffordshire. (Bernard Lowry)

a network of hilltop radio stations was constructed by the government. Among the radio stations in this region were ones at Romsley in Worcestershire and The Wrekin in Shropshire. Both or either of these networks would be used in an emergency with the one providing a backup to the other.

As in the Second World War, there was to be a regional organization but this time it would take control during and after a nuclear attack. The West Midlands was again Region No 9, with a War Room constructed in the 1950s in Shirley, Birmingham. Additionally there was an anti-aircraft operations room in Wylde Green, Sutton Coldfield. By the end of the 1950s both of these had become redundant. At the start of the 1960s, to replace the war room, a regional seat of government (RSG) was constructed in the tunnels at Drakelow in Worcestershire. (Drakelow had been a shadow factory in the Second World War; see chapter 1.) In the 1980s the bunker at Swynnerton in Staffordshire (see above for earlier use) became a subsidiary RSG for the eastern part of the West Midlands, with Drakelow remaining the main RSG and also covering the western part of the region.

As well as regional HQs local authorities had to provide and maintain emergency HQs. In some cases these were buildings identified and reserved for this purpose whilst in others they were the basement of the town hall or other such building. For example, in Hereford prior to 1974 what had previously been cells under the Magistrates' Court were used; in Staffordshire the basement of the County

9/7 Repeater Station, Whitecrest, Sandwell, West Midlands. (Colin Jones)

Building in Stafford was used and in Warwickshire, again prior to 1974, Wylde Green was used (see above for previous use). If a new building was constructed it would contain an underground bunker for this purpose; an example being the new county hall built on the outskirts of Worcester in the mid 1970s following the re-organisation of local government.

The tunnels at Drakelow remain although not often open to the public. The building containing the Shirley war room was demolished in 2005 but the bunkers at Swynnerton still remain. Local authorities' emergency control centres are also often still in existence being used as store rooms in many cases. Generally they are not accessible to the public.

Fire Services

Prior to 1938 fire services were organised on a local basis, often at the parish level. During the First World War many were still using horses although most were in the process of moving to motorized vehicles. Initially there was no attempt to co-ordinate the provision of fire services and local fire brigades were left to do their best after bombing raids. They also had to deal with any aircraft crashes in their area and with fires or explosions in the many munitions factories that had been established (see chapter 1). Fire brigades were not helped by their men initially not being exempt from call-up although this did change later in the war following the bombing of London. The onset of bombing raids by aircraft resulted in some co-ordination of fire services from 1917 onwards. This was first applied to London and then later to the West Midlands (and other parts of the country) with the chief fire officer of Birmingham being appointed as the co-ordinator. This structure remained in place until 1921.

In the 1920s, following a Royal Commission report on fire services, the Home Office appointed an honorary Fire Adviser (in the 1930s he was taken onto the staff). Early in the 1930s he pointed out that there would need to be an expansion of the fire services if there was another war. A departmental review of fire services was then undertaken in 1935/36 and the first result was the establishment of a Fire Brigades Division in the Home Office in late 1936. In February 1937 they issued their first circular to local fire authorities which asked them to consider the fire risks resulting from a war and to draw up a scheme of fire precautions. They were to consider the numbers of auxiliary firemen and fire stations they would need.

In 1938 a Fire Brigades Act was passed which made the boroughs and urban and rural districts responsible for fire services. This was the first time that fire services had become a compulsory local authority

9/8 Regional HQ of the NFS, Pirehill, near Stone, Staffordshire. (Bernard Lowry)

As a result, the fire services were nationalized in 1941 and the AFS and fire brigades were merged under one command. The new National Fire Service (NFS) was organized into 33 areas, four of which covered the West Midlands: Birmingham & District; the counties of Hereford, Warwick and Worcester (HQ at Bevere Manor, near Worcester); Shropshire and Staffordshire (HQ at Pirehill House, Stone); and Wolverhampton & District. The fire service remained nationalised until 1948 when the service was returned to the counties and county boroughs although in a few cases, such as Worcester, the county borough amalgamated its service with the county.

To provide water when mains supplies were disrupted, many water tanks were erected during the Second World War. In residential areas these were often steel tanks located either on spare ground or on the road. Larger tanks were erected to help fire fighting at factories that were important to the war effort. These tanks were constructed using a variety of materials, and the remains of a large concrete tank can be seen in St Godwald's Road,

service (apart from in London). The Act gave the new fire authorities two years to become fully up to strength. The Act also formalized the Auxiliary Fire Service (AFS) although recruitment to it had begun as a result of the earlier circular. At the beginning of the Second World War the AFS was mobilized, the men often being paid less than they received in their previous full-time occupation. Buildings were taken over to house the crew and their trailer pump. Often these buildings were in a poor state and the men, many of whom were tradesmen, had to get their quarters habitable. The local authority had to acquire vehicles to pull the trailer pumps and such vehicles were often old private cars; in London they were often taxis. There is some evidence that the AFS in a few cases erected their own station. This was possible during the period of the phoney war as bombing did not start till June 1940.

Co-ordination between the AFS and the fire brigades often did not work well as was shown after some bombing raids.

9/9 1939 Fire Station, Worcester. (Colin Jones)

Bromsgrove. Other sources of water would often be indicated by the letters EWS (emergency water supply) painted on a nearby wall or other flat surface.

To further help fire fighting a system of fire watchers was set up in 1940 in premises employing over 30 persons. Their purpose was to detect fires and summon assistance. In 1941 the system was formalized as the Fire Guard with employees having to do compulsory service for so many hours a month. In residential areas street fire parties were formed with similar responsibilities. Both systems did help in the early warning of fires, usually from incendiary bombs, thus limiting damage. To assist in fire fighting at this level a stirrup pump had been produced from 1938 onwards and these were issued in great numbers. They could be very useful in containing fires started by incendiaries if they were used quickly at the seat of the fire. Stirrup pumps could also be purchased by the public and they were encouraged to do this.

With the onset of the Cold War, in 1950 a decision was made that, in the event of war, fire services would be immediately nationalized and organized into

9/10 Former AFS station, Tenbury Wells, Worcestershire. (Colin Jones)

9/11 Emergency water tank, St Godwalds Road, Bromsgrove, Worcestershire. (Colin Jones)

twelve regions, one of which would be the West Midlands. A Chief Fire Officer designate was appointed for each region who undertook voluntary co-ordination work in case of an emergency. During the 1950s, fire brigades held exercises, with other civil defence personnel, simulating the effects of atomic warfare. Such exercises continued until the late 1960s. In 1969 the AFS, which had continued on a part-time basis since the end of the Second World War, was disbanded as no longer required due to the Nuclear Non-proliferation Treaty. In the 1970s and 1980s the fire services continued to be involved in the planning of civil defence through their links with the Home Office, which remained in overall control of policy on civil defence including fire services. One policy promulgated in the 1970s was to disperse many firemen and their appliances out of the major towns if a nuclear attack looked imminent. They would then be available for rescue services after the attack. Obviously this required sufficient warning. Most fire stations had a siren on their roof, often left from the Second World War, which would be sounded to give warning of a nuclear attack. The Green Goddess fire appliances, which had been purchased in the 1950s for use by the AFS, were retained by the Home Office after the AFS was disbanded in 1968 so that they could be used after an attack. It is only in this century that the Green Goddesses were finally pensioned off.

A number of fire stations still occupy the buildings that were erected for the new brigades in the late 1930s but some earlier buildings remain. Other buildings are more modern having been constructed in the years since the Second World War.

Many buildings occupied by the AFS during the war also remain, having reverted to their previous use. However there is now no sign of their use as fire stations. The remains of the occasional emergency water tank can sometimes still be seen. Other remnants of the Second World War are the fire hydrants located on bridges above rivers, streams and canals. These were constructed so that water could be easily obtained to fight fires, it being recognised that the water in street tanks (c.5,000 gallons) would not last very long if there was a conflagration.

RAF AND US AIRFIELDS

10

Military fighter aircraft were first based in the West Midlands in the middle of the First World War. To counter the Zeppelin menace, No 38 (Home Defence) Squadron of the Royal Flying Corps had been formed at Castle Bromwich in July 1916, operating four detachments at small landing fields located at Great Barr, Chasetown, Kingswinford and Perton. The squadron HQ moved to Leicestershire in September 1916. Fortunately there were only four Zeppelin raids on the Midlands (see chapter 9) during the war although no interceptions by the slow and obsolete squadron aircraft took place.

The formation of the Royal Air Force on 1 April 1918, replacing the Royal Flying Corps, and the establishment just over a month later of Home Commands (No 3 was the Midlands Area) reflected the growing importance of this new and revolutionary force. On the Western Front aerial reconnaissance using cameras was becoming highly developed, the long-range heavy bomber had arrived, and the Hindenburg Line was breached in September 1918 using heavy air support. The demand for trained aircrews would see airfields established in the Midlands, and aircraft manufacturers such as Austin at Longbridge, producing the successful SE5a fighter amongst others, had their own small airfields.

Amongst the training airfields Tern Hill in Shropshire was established in late 1916, becoming No 13 Training Depot. Types as large as the Handley Page 0/400 bomber were on hand to train crews. Accommodation for personnel was in wooden hutting, with smaller aircraft accommodated in canvas Bessonneau hangars until 1919 when a fire destroyed many buildings along with four of the

10/1 A First World War general service shed (hangar) at Monkmoor, Shrewsbury.
(Bernard Lowry)

heavy bombers. In 1922 the site was sold for civilian use. Flying training began at Shawbury airfield in 1917 with wooden buildings and hangars along its western edge. Like Tern Hill the site was closed after the war and the site cleared.

Not too far away, at Monkmoor on the outskirts of Shrewsbury, the Observer's School of Reconnaissance and Aerial Photography was established, briefly, in 1918. Two general service sheds with Belfast truss roofs were provided together with personnel accommodation. The site was used during the Second World War for salvage work by the RAF No 34 Maintenance Unit (MU).

Also in Shrewsbury a depot was established at Harlescott in 1918, between the Whitchurch road and the railway line, for the repair of aircraft and their engines. After the war it was used for the storage and repair of RAF motor transport, and married quarters were built nearby. The site closed in 1932. In the Cold War the buildings were used as a buffer depot (see chapter 3).

By November 1933 the RAF's strength had sunk to only 850 aircraft. The deteriorating situation in Europe prompted calls for the revitalising of the RAF and in November 1934 an expansion programme was launched. In 1936 four RAF Commands were established as part of the programme: Fighter, Bomber, Training and Coastal. At the outbreak of war, the RAF's strength had increased to 3,550 first-line aircraft, with a grand total of 9,343 aircraft plus 174,000 men. By January 1945 these figures had reached 8,400 first line aircraft, with 55,000 aircraft

in total, and more than a million personnel, both male and female, at home and overseas. The West Midlands would make a significant contribution during this period to the essential job of training thousands of aircrew and airmen and airwomen.

The expansion programme's results remain with us in the form of such airfields as Shawbury, their handsome buildings still in use. A number of national civil engineering firms were established on the strength of the RAF contracts, including McAlpines, which had been formed only two years before it began to build Cosford airfield. Suitable hangars, to accommodate ever-larger aircraft, had to be designed and

10/2 The elegant architecture of the RAF's expansion period: the officers' mess at RAF Shawbury, Shropshire. (Bernard Lowry)

10/3 One of the large, hipped, C-type hangars at Bramcote, Warwickshire. The design also included lateral offices, seen here, whilst the hangar doors were hollow so that, in the event of conflict, they could be filled with gravel to make them blast proof. (Steve Carvell)

built but their impact on the countryside was given careful consideration, resulting in natural materials such as brick, slate and tile being used wherever possible. But the designs were slow to build and expensive. The large C-type hangar was the first of the new designs, but they were demanding in terms of labour and materials. The D-type hangar was designed for storage on Maintenance Units (such as Cosford and Tern Hill), the similar J and K designs were for the use of operational aircraft and aircraft storage respectively. Another range of designs, using a curved concrete or steel frame, influenced ironically by patents of the German Junkers firm, could be concealed under a covering of grass: these were the E, L and Lamella types usually seen on Aircraft Storage (e.g. Lichfield) and Maintenance Units (e.g. Cosford). Roughly circular grass airfields (in order that aircraft could take off into a prevailing wind) were the order of the day, with station buildings grouped in a semi-circle, storage hangars being further afield. From 1936 there was a call for large transportable hangars, the

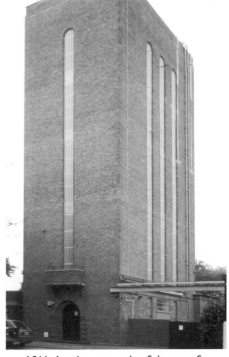

10/4 Another example of the care for architectural detail on RAF expansion airfields: the station water tower at RAF Shawbury. (Bernard Lowry)

10/5 A common sight on many RAF airfields was the Bellman hangar. This example, at Tern Hill in Shropshire, was erected after an attack by a Junkers Ju 88 damaged beyond repair one of the large C-type hangars on the station. Behind, are postwar barrack buildings. (Bernard Lowry)

10/8 A K-type hangar at High Ercall in Shropshire with a machine gun pillbox added for airfield defence. (Bernard Lowry)

10/9 A B1-type hangar still in use on the former RAF Seighford site in Staffordshire. (Bernard Lowry)

Bellman being introduced at this time. This was soon considered to be not big enough for the job so the T (models 1-3) was introduced.

On very late pre-war stations, for example Halfpenny Green in Staffordshire and Bramcote in Warwickshire, airfield station buildings were grouped together, although this made them vulnerable to bombing attack. Amongst the last airfields to be constructed in the West Midlands before the outbreak of war was the large Aircraft Storage Unit (ASU) at Lichfield. Airfields built during the war had their personnel and technical buildings (including hangars) dispersed to avoid catastrophic casualties and damage from bombing attack: the grouping of buildings on expansion airfields was seen as a vulnerable liability. The war also saw new designs of hangar such as the large Callender-Hamilton and the B1-type for bomber stations, whilst the Navy used the S-type, Mainhill and Pentad designs. The 1920s Hinaidi design was resurrected and examples were erected at Madley in Herefordshire. At some airfields the concrete floors of hangars provided handy rollerskating rinks for off-duty airmen and women!

10/10 A design, with the B, commonly found on bomber stations was the T2 hangar, this example being at Hixon in Staffordshire. (Bernard Lowry)

10/7 Typical of the hangars built on Aircraft Storage and Maintenance Units before the start of the Second World War are these three at RAF Cosford, Shropshire. Their grass-covered design was to make them less conspicuous from the air. Although appearing to be identical there are three different designs here. That on the left is an L-type, that on the right an E-type whilst the central one is a Lamella hangar. (Bernard Lowry)

10/6 An aerial view taken in the 1960s of Honeybourne (Worcestershire) airfield's technical site. The airfield was, from 1941, a Bomber Command Operational Training Unit base. The runways were to the left, off the picture but the perimeter track, connecting the five hangars (four T2s and one J-type), can be seen snaking towards the commencement of each of the three interconnecting runways. The watch office (control tower) was to the left of the large J-type hangar. The three-pointed star shape was part of the airfield's defence system: three FC Construction (also known as 'mushroom' or 'Oakington') pillboxes, each connected to the other by a trench. (WHEAS)

10/11 The relatively rare Callender-Hamilton hangar, this one being on the former airfield at Madley in Herefordshire. (Mick Wilks)

To ease the burden on busy airfields during the war relief and satellite landing grounds were created, these having minimum facilities. Satellites (SLGs) were part of the complement of a larger, parent airfield and the former might have a number of small 'Robin' hangars on site. Relief landing grounds (RLGs) were designed to take the pressure off over-burdened local airfields and would have open-ended Blister hangars to give a degree of protection to aircraft.

In addition, large non-flying Maintenance Units were established for general storage, the principal sites being at Hartlebury and Stafford. Hartlebury was constructed in 1938 whilst work on the 362-acre site at Stafford was begun in December 1939 by the firm of McAlpines. The severe winter delayed the work, the first airmen arriving in April 1940. Land at Trentham Park was requisitioned in 1941 as a dispersed site for motor transport (MT) storage for 16 MU at RAF Stafford. The work at Trentham was directed by the Superintendent of Engineering at the Air Ministry Directorate based at Tunstall Hall near Market Drayton. Other MUs were established for bomb and fuel storage (see chapter 1) and Group HQs such as that at Buntingsdale Hall near Market Drayton were set up. The latter was purchased in 1939 when it housed No 20 Group, part of Training Command, and its responsibilities underwent various changes; in the middle of the war it housed No 25 Group controlling eleven training squadrons stretching from Exeter to Dumfries. The Group's equipment probably included the large radio station close to the Hall. Although largely unsung, Training Command played an immensely vital role in supplying trained

10/12 One of the hangar designs used by the Royal Navy was the Pentad with, in the foreground, a Handcraft hut at the former RNAS HMS Godwit, originally RAF Hinstock airfield, Shropshire. (Bernard Lowry)

10/13 Representative of other specialized RAF buildings is this double turret trainer on the former RAF Tilstock site in Shropshire, now used as offices. (Bernard Lowry)

aircrews to operational squadrons to keep pace with their growth, but also to make up for the terrible losses suffered by Bomber Command. The RAF was also involved in the 'wireless war' (see chapter 4).

Aerial landings by German aircraft and paratroops on continental airfields in 1940 led to a fear of similar tactics being employed against British airfields. Airfields also held vital stores of war material. A policy for the defence of airfields was immediately put in place (see chapter 6), and Fig 5 shows a typical airfield defence scheme. The advent of enemy bombing attacks on airfields, firstly by day and then at night, led to the use of decoys airfields (see chapter 8).

Despite the British climate and the advent of heavier aircraft, it was only from 1939 that concrete runways began to be introduced, the 'ideal' design for the RAF being an equilateral triangle, whilst Royal Naval Air Stations had their own designs (a feature that also extended to their airfield buildings). On some smaller airfields the use of grass surfaces neverthe-

less continued up to the end of the war. Waterlogged grass surfaces continued to impose severe problems on the operation of airfields, a situation improved by the use of metal matting (often seen post war reused as farm fencing) to reinforce the grassed edges of concrete runways. To control the movement of aircraft on the runways the RAF produced a number of different designs of watch office (referred to by the Royal Navy on their airfields as control towers), their designs reflecting the date and type of airfield they were designed to serve. The number and size of airfields led to a massive demand for hutting, for a large airfield could contain several hundred buildings, and the RAF had priority for Nissen huts for the accommodation of airmen and women. Lightweight brick buildings were erected on the tech-

10/14 The smallest hangar used by the RAF was the Robin. Quite elaborate camouflage schemes had been drawn up by the eminent architect Sir Hugh Casson, serving with the RAF in the Second World War, to conceal these relatively small and isolated structures. This example, once one of many serving RAF Shawbury in Shropshire, retains traces of a brick red paint scheme, perhaps to make it resemble a farm building. The hangar doors are on the right elevation. (Bernard Lowry)

10/15 The rare 'fort'-type watch office at Cosford in Shropshire, the design originating in 1934. (Bernard Lowry)

nical sites. A range of other materials for hutting was also used, including corrugated asbestos, plywood, plasterboard and concrete panels. However, conditions for airmen, especially on partially completed airfields, were invariably primitive, they often having to make do with tents in muddy fields, with little hot water and very basic sanitary arrangements.

In the West Midlands area Shropshire had the lion's share of new wartime airfields, the majority being in the relatively flat and sparsely populated northern part of the county. However, the concentration of airfields was dangerous and there were many crashes on the higher land in fog or low cloud. The prominent landmark of The Wrekin was given a beacon to warn aircraft flying from the airfields around its base. So vital was the production of food that crops were often grown on the land between the runways and a popular station

pastime was the fattening of a pig or pigs to supply extra bacon supplies to the cookhouse. The larger airfields would develop into complex 'townships' with boreholes for water, emergency generators, sewage disposal tanks, operations blocks, control towers, and specialist synthetic training aids such as the dome trainer. Aircraft guns of different calibres were tested in large gun butts and on bomber stations there were detached bomb stores. With so many young men and women working together or close to towns, even if their individual camps were separated, the need for contraceptives and fear of disease was catered for by the station's 'prophylactic store'.

Although in the Second World War the area's airfields were mainly involved in storage, maintenance or training, a number of airfields were involved in aggressive

10/18 Control tower of the former RNAS HMS Godwit in Shropshire, a design dating from 1942. It has now been converted into a house. (Bernard Lowry)

warfare. The night fighter airfields of Tern Hill, High Ercall, Bagington and Honiley are mentioned in chapter 8. The bomber training airfields of Lichfield, Hixon, Seighford, Bramcote, Tilstock, Gaydon, Wellesbourne Mountford, Honeybourne, Peplow and Pershore were involved in either dropping leaflets ('Nickels') or sometimes bombs over enemy territory. Honiley, after night fighting operations declined, carried out 'Ranger' operations against enemy locomotives. Other airfields were on the receiving end: Pershore, Shawbury and Tern Hill were bombed in the early part of the war, the last losing one hangar in the attack. Other airfields had famous, if short term, residents. The daughter of the Polish patriot Marshall Pilsudski, Jadwiga Pilsudska, was an ATA pilot at Cosford. The

10/17 Hixon, Staffordshire. A bomber station watch office whose design originated in 1941. The building is now used as an office. (Bernard Lowry)

French writer Pierre Clostermann was at Rednal and Mountford Bridge undergoing training in order to fly Spitfires, whilst Group Captain Leonard Cheshire VC, after completing two tours of duty on heavy bombers, spent time at 24 MU, RAF Stoke Heath, attached to Tern Hill airfield ferrying

10/16 The influence of art deco domestic architecture is evident in the design of the watch office at Bramcote, this design originating in 1939. (Steve Carvell)

10/19 The airmens' mess at the former RAF Bramcote (now Gamecock Barracks) airfield in Warwickshire, again reflecting the influence of 1930s art deco architecture. (Bernard Lowry)

Halifax bombers in 1942. Atcham airfield, handed to the USAAF 8th AF in 1942, was the northernmost outpost of this mighty war machine. Fig 12 shows the location of all the known airfields in the region.

The end of the war saw the running down of most RAF stations. At some airfields former living accommodation was taken over by displaced persons, such as Polish families on the former WAAF site at Tilstock (the bath house being converted into a chapel). Some such as Gaydon and Shawbury remained in military use, this pair being reserved for V-bomber use (the A53 at the latter being diverted to cater for a lengthened runway to take the V-bombers). Municipal airfields such as Elmdon, taken over during the war, were returned to civilian use; Elmdon itself grew to become Birmingham's international airport.

To train the large numbers of RAF ground crew and also certain types of aircrew, three large training camps were established in the region: at Bridgnorth, Hednesford and Hereford. All would make a massive contribution to the wartime expansion of the RAF. A significant start in the training of RAF technicians had already been made in August 1938 with the opening at RAF Cosford of the No 2 School of Technical Training. This was provided with its own impressive barracks, the Fulton Block, still in use today. Over 70,000 engine and airframe mechanics and armourers were trained here during the war.

RAF Bridgnorth

Opened in May 1940, this was intended to house up to 2,800 airmen in wooden hutting with two T2 hangars used as drill sheds. It was initially used as a transit camp and kitting out centre, dealing with the Czech, Polish, Belgian and Dutch airmen who had fled to the UK after the fall of France. By June 1940 it was able to begin training recruits for the RAF. Between June 1941 and Sept 1942 it was used for WAAF training. It then became No 1 Elementary Air Navigation School training bomber navigators. Immediately after the war the site accommodated No 7 School of Recruits Training Centre and it carried on performing this task until closure in 1963. The camp was dismantled and, as at Hednesford, a country park now occupies the site.

RAF Hednesford

Built just before the outbreak of war, in the Second World War it was the RAF's No 6 School of Technical Training, and was

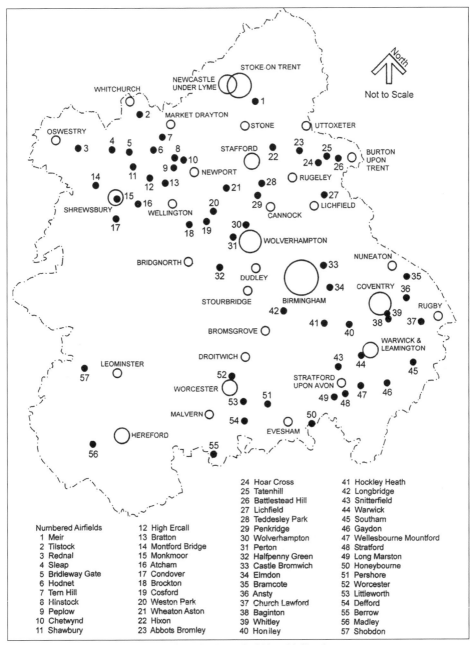

Fig 12 Airfields in the West Midlands

Numbered Airfields
1 Meir
2 Tilstock
3 Rednal
4 Sleap
5 Bridleway Gate
6 Hodnet
7 Tern Hill
8 Hinstock
9 Peplow
10 Chetwynd
11 Shawbury

12 High Ercall
13 Bratton
14 Montford Bridge
15 Monkmoor
16 Atcham
17 Condover
18 Brockton
19 Cosford
20 Weston Park
21 Wheaton Aston
22 Hixon
23 Abbots Bromley

24 Hoar Cross
25 Tatenhill
26 Battlestead Hill
27 Lichfield
28 Teddesley Park
29 Penkridge
30 Wolverhampton
31 Perton
32 Halfpenny Green
33 Castle Bromwich
34 Elmdon
35 Bramcote
36 Ansty
37 Church Lawford
38 Baginton
39 Whitley
40 Honiley

41 Hockley Heath
42 Longbridge
43 Snitterfield
44 Warwick
45 Southam
46 Gaydon
47 Wellesbourne Mountford
48 Stratford
49 Long Marston
50 Honeybourne
51 Pershore
52 Worcester
53 Littleworth
54 Defford
55 Berrow
56 Madley
57 Shobdon

located at the southern end of Cannock Chase. Like the Army personnel on the Chase its Second World War servicemen lived in wooden huts, although a Bellman and a Hinaidi hangar were provided for instruction accommodation. It was unique in having a synagogue for the use of Jewish servicemen. Postwar, it became part of the National Service system, in 1950 becoming No 11 School of Recruit Training, 80,000 RAF men passing through (including one of the authors of this book, who spent eight weeks doing basic training there). It closed in 1956 but was almost immediately re-used to house refugees from the 1956 Hungarian Uprising. Demolished by the 1970s, the fragmentary remains now form part of a country park.

RAF Hereford

Opened in 1939 near the hamlet of Credenhill, and, apart from the ubiquitous wood and brick hutting, it had nine Hinaidi hangars for instruction and other purposes. It became No 11 School of Technical Training, also training Polish and Czech

10/20 The somewhat sinister entrance to the Cold War nuclear bomber base at Gaydon in Warwickshire. (Bernard Lowry)

airmen. At its peak in 1941 it contained seven thousand trainees, learning various trades. Arguably its most famous occupant was Bill Wyman of The Rolling Stones who was here in 1955 before passing out as a 'Clerk Progress'. In 1999, the RAF having left in 1994, the SAS took over the site, moving from the Stirling Lines barracks at Hereford.

US airstrips

In addition to the US 8th Air Force airfield at Atcham (originally a British airfield but handed over to the US in June 1942) there were other, smaller flying facilities used by the US forces. To facilitate courier and communications work at the many US facilities a number of small airstrips were established, often known as 'Cub Strips' (named after the civilian version of the Piper L-4 aircraft), most of the aircraft belonging to Field Artillery Units; when on combat duty the aircraft were used as air observation posts. Crews of the paired aircraft were accommodated in eight-men bell tents and were provided with a Jeep. Aircraft used were the Piper L-4 Grasshopper and the slightly larger Stinson L-5 Reliant, this latter type performing most of the liaison work of the US 9th Air Force, attached to higher level HQs of the Army ground forces. Airstrips were established close to the artillery units on fields or sports pitches and hence little if any evidence of this activity remains today. By October 1944 most of these airstrips had been abandoned and by May 1945 virtually all US aircraft had left the UK.

ARMY CAMPS

The British Army's use of pre-fabricated hutting for barracks and field hospitals dates back to the Crimean War. These huts were of wood but later hutting also made use of brick and concrete blocks and towards the end of the nineteenth century corrugated, galvanised roofing panels appeared. Attention was also given to clean drinking water supplies and hygienic sewage disposal. The unprecedented expansion of the Army at the time of the First World War led to the building of new camps, often designed to each hold an infantry division of up to 15,000 men. Well-drained ground with good communication facilities were chosen and standard layouts adopted. In the West Midlands large camps were built on Cannock Chase, at Park Hall near Oswestry and at Prees Heath near Whitchurch, with others at Lichfield, Sutton Coldfield, Worcester and Malvern.

Before the start of the war there was countrywide barrack accommodation for 175,000 soldiers, so the creation of an army of a million men at the outbreak of war clearly created an accommodation problem. At first men were accommodated in tents until a nationwide network of large camps was completed. Cannock Chase, for example, was chosen because occupation of the land would not affect food production: the site was well drained, it was positioned between areas with large populations, and was also close to roads and railways. An army of carpenters was recruited to construct the wooden and stove-heated barrack huts. By the beginning of 1915 the capacity of all of the country's camps had almost reached the one million figure, this rising to 1,750,000 men by Autumn 1917.

On the Chase two large camps were built, one near Brocton and the other near Rugeley. Each could accommodate an infantry division plus its artillery (a combined total of 40,000 men), although in the event a division was never quartered on the Chase. In the early part of the war they served mainly as transit camps, and were later used to accommodate different Schools of Instruction, such as that for the building of fieldworks and other fortifications. In addition, a 1,000-bed hospital was built at Brindley Heath. To supply water for the camps and hospital three deep shafts were dug on the high ground at Brocton Camp, water being pumped to a huge elevated tank, capable of holding thousands of gallons. Electricity for the pumps, and also for the lighting of the camps, was generated by a large powerhouse. New roads, a sewage disposal system, rifle ranges and a camp railway, employing at least five locomotives, were built. To cater for the soldiers' needs a YMCA, a cinema, banks and even a branch of WH Smith were on site to relieve the monotony of

11/1 Representative of the bleak nature of hutted camps in the first half of the twentieth century is this photograph of the Royal Artillery camp at Park Hall near Oswestry in Shropshire, taken at the time of the 1952 Coronation. The prehistoric hillfort of Old Oswestry (used in the First World War for troop training) is in the background. The writer Barbara Pym was a catering volunteer at the camp in 1940. (Wayne Cocroft)

life for the quarter of a million men who passed through the camps, many sadly never seeing home again. (The remains of a small camp also exist near the present SAS barracks at Credenhill, used as a hostel for workers at the former First World War Army Ordnance Depot at Credenhill.) After the end of the war, camp build-ings were removed and much of the area reverted to scrub or disappeared under large coniferous plantations. In the Second World War the Chase returned to mili-tary activity, a large swathe being used to test tanks and part being used as a Home Guard grenade range close to the former camp sewage plant by Milford Common.

11/2 The foundations of the huge, elevated First World War water tower on Cannock Chase in Staffordshire, a memorial stone marks the site. Behind the photographer is the cutting for one of the railway lines that served the camps on the Chase. (Bernard Lowry)

114 Examples of the once ubiquitous Nissen hut survive at the former Nesscliffe ordnance depot in Shropshire. Small blast walls have been added, presumably as a degree of protection should there have been an explosion on the site. (Bernard Lowry)

A small practice bombing range was also built for the RAF near Anson's Bank. In the Cold War the elevated position of the Chase afforded an ideal site for one of the government's 'Backbone' reinforced communications towers at Pye Green (see chapter 9).

The need for vast quantities of portable hutting in the First World War led to the invention of the Nissen hut, designed by a Captain Nissen of the Royal Engineers, in 1916. Although the hut would prove to be ubiquitous, especially in the next war, it proved to be only semi-portable as it was difficult to align bolt holes for re-erection elsewhere. The standard design (27ft x16ft) could accommodate one NCO and seven other ranks. A larger version with windows was used for messes and other communal purposes.

As camp building got under way after the Munich crisis of September 1938 there was a trend towards smaller and more dispersed camps than in the previous war,

and the appearance of new structures such as 'spider huts', a block of six huts grouped around a central corridor. These were centrally heated, and permanently but lightly built by civilian contractors for six NCOs and 120 men. The advent of war in 1939 and the influx of men from continental armies fleeing to the UK led to another crisis in accommodation as in the previous war, the men often being accommodated in tents with their officers in requisitioned houses. Military vehicles were often stored in the parkland of large houses or on closed by-passes such as that at Church Stretton.

The cutting off of Britain's pre-war timber supplies from the Baltic countries in 1940 led to the need for new designs and alternative materials, the work being sponsored by the Ministry of Works. Corrugated asbestos, breezeblock, terracotta, tarpaper, plasterboard, plywood and concrete panel on a reinforced concrete frame were all used to create tens of thousands of huts on camps. The First World War Nissen came back and was used by the Army, RAF and US forces, together with a new design for storage, the large Romney hut. The Handcraft hut was another commonly found design using corrugated asbestos for the angular roof design. The Navy tended to use its own designs for hutting, again with corrugated asbestos roofing. Housing for key workers near the large new and ordnance depots (such as that at Donnington in Shropshire) and ordnance factories (such as that at Swynnerton in Staffordshire) used flat or slightly sloping concrete roofs. Similar housing for key workers was also built at Drakelow and Stone, near Kidderminster, at Blackpole, Worcester, and at Redditch. Concrete was also used in finishes such as staircases. To house the large numbers of workers directed into new factories workers' hostels were built, such as those that surrounded Swynnerton and named after illustrious naval captains such as Drake Hall, now the site of a women's prison.

After the war much of the hutting was sold off and, on still-used military sites, replaced by more permanent hutting. However the Nissen would last well into the Cold War. As the RAF shrank, so some of their airfield accommodation was taken over by the Army and modernised. For example, the Army's Gamecock Barracks is on the former Bramcote airfield site in Warwickshire; Tern Hill in Shropshire is now used by the Army; and the SAS have taken over the former RAF Hereford (see chapter 10) at Credenhill in Herefordshire.

11/5 British-supplied Romney huts for the US 83rd Ordnance Sub Depot now in commercial use near Wem in Shropshire. (Bernard Lowry)

Barracks

Two of the large Victorian barracks built in the West Midlands remain in use by the military. These are Copthorne Barracks near Shrewsbury and Whittington in Staffordshire. Budbrooke Barracks, in Warwick, were demolished in the 1960s and all that remains of Norton Barracks near Worcester is the Keep, now split into flats. The less populous county of Herefordshire had a Militia Barracks in the county town, now used by the County Record Office. The county regiments' contributions were significant: in the First World War, for example, over 47,000 men joined the Warwickshire Regiment, of which almost a quarter were killed. In the next war the regiment served in Europe, the Middle and Far East, India and in home defence.

In addition to permanent barracks many temporary hutted camps emerged during the Second World War, whilst large country houses provided emergency accommodation, especially after the Dunkirk evacuation, for officers, with men billeted in tented accommodation in the grounds. Examples of the latter are Hewell Grange (now a prison) and Bentley Manor (destroyed by fire some years ago), both near Redditch.

Whittington Barracks, Staffordshire

This is still occupied by the Army for training and retains many of its original buildings. The building of such county barracks originated from the Cardwell Reforms of 1870, under which it was proposed that new barracks would support two pairs of county regiments, with one pair serving at home and the other overseas on a rotating basis. There would also be a Militia Battalion *in situ*. In 1881 the 38th and 80th Regiments became the 1st and 2nd South Staffordshire Regiment and the 64th and 98th became the 1st and 2nd North Staffordshire Regiment, and these moved into the newly completed barracks, which also contained married quarters and a hospital. For the soldiers' moral wellbeing there was a garrison church. The exterior wall was lightly defensible and the magazine was in a crenellated, keep-like building. In the First World War service battalions were raised here to be trained, and they replaced the Regular Army garrison. Immediately before the

Second World War it was the HQ and home to two regiments of the 2nd (AA) Brigade, Royal Artillery. After the early departure of the brigade, in September 1942, the barracks accommodated the US Army 10th Replacement Depot, and by the end of 1944 200,000 GIs had passed through it. To cope with the expansion, temporary huts and tents were erected on adjacent land. The Replacement Depot gained notoriety for bullying and the imposition of cruel punishments for breaches of regulations, the situation becoming so grave that at the conclusion of the war the commanding officer, Lieutenant Colonel Killian, was court-martialled. The penalty imposed on him was generally considered to be too lenient when compared with

113 The imposing, nineteenth-century keep at Whittington Barracks, Staffordshire, still in military use. In the Second World War the barracks was used by the US Army as a Replacement Depot. (Bernard Lowry)

the harsh punishments imposed on lesser ranks. The controversy did, however, lead to the shaking-up of the US courts martial system. In the post-war period the old married quarters were demolished and replaced. In 1959 the barracks became the home of the newly formed Staffordshire Regiment, then becoming the Mercian Brigade Depot. It became the home of the Army Training Regiment (Lichfield), training recruits for the Royal Corps of Signals and the Royal Engineers, and is now the HQ of the Mercian Regiment, which is equipped with new, modern barracks as well as the modernized Victorian buildings. Outside the barracks is an interesting museum devoted to the Staffordshire Regiment, which, of course, no longer exists.

Drill Halls

The establishment of county volunteer companies in the nineteenth century was regularized by the formation of the Territorial Force in 1908 which was, in turn, replaced by the creation of the Territorial Army in 1921. The new county-based force took over existing drill halls, adapted existing premises which had had previous uses (that at Upton-on-Severn had been a warehouse), or built new drill halls which also included Riding Schools for the Yeomanry (cavalry volunteer regiments). In the First World War the halls acted as recruiting and mobilization centres but after the war enthusiasm for volunteer soldiering faded. This picked up in the 1930s when the country was faced

with the rise of fascism and it is believed that over 200 new drill halls were built countrywide in that decade, the favoured military building style being an elegant neo-Georgian style. The TA, like the Regular Army, had to change with the increasingly complex nature of warfare, but despite the assignment to the Territorial Associations of the responsibility for the country's anti-aircraft defence, which included searchlight duties, insufficient funds were diverted to the TA. Only a limited number of halls could accommodate the new 3.7" anti-aircraft guns for the necessary drill.

On the outbreak of war the Regular and Territorial Armies merged, TA Associations taking over in 1940 the role of equipping the Home Guard. Not surprisingly the Home Guard would frequently use drill halls as their headquarters and for storing ammunition and heavier weaponry such as the Spigot Mortar. Drill Halls also often formed the Home Guard's local 'keep' and place of last resort in their local defence schemes (see chapter 6).

Although the TA is now in a much-reduced form it survives and makes use of pre- and post-war halls. However, in many parts of the country the older drill halls are disappearing. For example, eleven of the sixteen in Shropshire have been demolished or have found other uses. In Kings Heath in Birmingham the neo-Georgian drill hall has been turned into flats; the castellated drill hall in Burslem, Stoke-on-Trent is now a keep-fit centre; whilst that at Ross-on-Wye is now a snooker hall.

THE ROYAL NAVY

Although the furthest of the UK regions from the sea, the Royal Navy located a number of training establishments, storage and production facilities as well as an experimental flying unit in the Midlands, where the relative remoteness of the area from occupied Europe allowed work to proceed without undue hindrance from the enemy. No naval establishments have been identified in the region prior to 1939, when the possibility of locating the Admiralty in Malvern as part of the government evacuation scheme seems to have influenced the arrival of other naval establishments. The presence of a number of armaments factories, together with good rail links to the west coast and the South Wales ports, appear to have been a further incentive to establish a naval presence here. The following naval establishments in the region have been identified so far.

Training Establishments

Basic, trade and flying training schools were located in the region by the navy. Despite the distance from the sea, naval tradition demanded that parade grounds became 'quarter-decks' and buildings would be given names derived from some of the great historic naval figures. Even the interiors of the buildings would be described in naval terms: corridors would become 'companion ways', walls 'bulkheads', toilets 'heads', canteens 'galleys', and so on. Every establishment would become a 'ship' and

leaving the establishment would entail waiting for the 'liberty boat' and 'going ashore', to give the new sailors at least some sense of being aboard a ship!

Possibly the largest naval training establishment in the region was HMS Duke in Malvern, where temporary office buildings constructed off St Andrew's Road for the Admiralty evacuation scheme were occupied throughout the war by this training school. Some 80,000 sailors were trained here before the base closed in March 1946. The 'ship' was commanded by Captain H. Spencer-Cooper and one of his trainee sailors was the late George Melly, the jazz singer, who recounted his experiences there in his book *Rum, Bum and Concertina*. The nearby New Pool, a relatively small private lake, gave the opportunity for water-borne training using cutters, whalers and skiffs, while the swimming pool at Malvern College was used to master water in another way. The weekly parade of sailors marching through the streets of Malvern, led by a Royal Marine band, is still remembered by many of the older residents of the town.

HMS Daedalus II was a naval artificer-training establishment. In May 1940, when the Germans began to occupy the Pas de Calais, it was quickly moved from Lympne airfield on the Kent coast to Clayton Hall, Newcastle-under-Lyme. A number of other properties in the vicinity were requisitioned and new buildings erected, including hutting and aircraft hangars, to accommodate the establishment. Students were trained in technical trades including airframes, engines, ordnance and electrical/radio work and both men and women would pass out as air fitters for service with the Fleet Air Arm. Cutters and whalers were available in Trentham Gardens for the students to learn waterborne skills. Over 4,000 personnel had been trained when HMS Daedalus II closed in December 1945. Clayton Hall is now a High School, and the gymnasium and chapel are the only other buildings remaining of this naval establishment.

A second training ship was established in April 1943 for WRNS technical training at Mill Meece, a few miles to the south of Clayton Hall and adjoining the Swynnerton ROF. Named HMS Fledgling, the establishment trained approximately 1,500 women as air mechanics or ordnance mechanics before closing in 1945. Over four hundred Canadian and two hundred Dutch ground crews also trained here.

The airfield at Hinstock, a former Satellite Landing Ground (SLG) near Childs Ercall in Shropshire, was transferred to the Admiralty in June 1943 to become HMS Godwit. Here, No 758 Squadron of the Naval Advanced Instrument Flying School would teach young Fleet Air Arm pilots, of limited experience, instrument flying and beam approach. Later, blind approach and other development work was also conducted here. A number of the hangars remain and the former control tower has been converted into a house. Until it closed in the summer of 1945, the SLG at Weston Park was used by the Navy as a satellite for Hinstock and was known as

HMS Godwit II. The Navy continued flying from Hinstock until February 1947, when the airfield was abandoned.

Postwar, Bramcote airfield was transferred from the RAF to the Royal Navy, becoming HMS Gamecock, where flying and mechanical training took place. During the war a basic training establishment had been established in the area, bearing the same name but little is known of this unit. The name lives on as the former airfield's buildings remain in use as the Army's Gamecock Barracks.

Experimental Flying

A Naval Air Section of the Fleet Air Arm was attached to Telecommunications Flying Unit at Defford airfield, operating and servicing naval aircraft used in connection with the development of radar, primarily Air to Surface Vessel Radar (ASV) for use by Coastal Command against the German U-Boats.

12/1 Now a school, Clayton Hall, Newcastle under Lyme, was the wartime headquarters of HMS Daedalus II, a naval artificer training establishment moved here from the Kent coast in 1940. Over 4,000 naval personnel were trained at the establishment before it closed in December 1945. (Bernard Lowry)

ALLIED FORCES 13

The occupation of much of Continental Europe and parts of Scandinavia by German forces following the campaigns of 1939-40, resulted in a number of the royal families and ministers of the occupied countries coming to Britain to establish governments-in-exile. With them came contingents of their defence forces to continue the fight. The West Midlands was a location chosen to accommodate, re-equip and train some of those allied military contingents. The strong emphasis on training aircrew in the West Midlands, referred to in chapter 10, also resulted in both foreign and Commonwealth air force personnel coming to the region for training. (An interesting aspect of the aircrew training in the West Midlands was that in 1942 a number of officers of the neutral Turkish Air Force were sent to Wolverhampton airfield for training by No 28 Elementary Flying Training School; this was arranged under the nose of Germany and with Winston Churchill's connivance.)

A second major 'friendly invasion' occurred when American troops arrived as part of Operation Bolero. Some two million American troops would eventually be moved through Britain during the latter part of the Second World War and, in an attempt to limit congestion on the already busy roads and railways, it was arranged to bring these troops in via the west coast ports. Thus, the majority were accommodated down the west side of Britain, moving south at the time of D-Day, whilst the British and Commonwealth ground forces were in general accommodated in the south and east of the country. The West Midlands would consequently see many American troops temporarily accommodated in the build-up for the D-Day landings and then housed for shorter periods as follow-up troops moved southwards through the region after D-Day. American Air Force personnel would also come into the Midlands for training and acclimatization purposes.

A third 'invasion' would come after the Americans had left with the arrival of returning Polish and other forces who, for political reasons, were unable to return to their homelands. They would occupy, often with their displaced families, vacated camps and hospitals until they could be permanently resettled in Britain or the Commonwealth.

French Forces

Following the unsuccessful Norwegian campaign and the evacuation from Dunkirk in the summer of 1940, Allied troops arrived in the region. In June 1940 Royal Engineers constructed a tented and guarded camp in the grounds of Trentham Park in Staffordshire for the arrival of 5,000 foreign troops. Amongst these were survivors of the 13th *demi-brigade* of the

French Foreign Legion (which contained at least one Englishman), *Chasseurs Alpins* and Polish Carpathian Lancers, these men being part of the ill-fated allied force sent to Norway in April 1940. In July French sailors were sent to Trentham following the seizure of French shipping moored in British ports after the French capitulation that month. The majority would be repatriated although a small number stayed at Trentham joining de Gaulle's Free French forces, eventually moving to Aldershot where French troops were concentrated. By the end of 1940 the camp was empty.

Amongst the French personnel evacuated from France were 200 youths, aged between 14 and 17 who, after a short stay in South Wales, were moved to No 5 House, Malvern College, in Worcestershire in February 1941. Using these boys as a nucleus, De Gaulle established an OCTU for *Cadets de la France Libre* that would train officers for the eventual return to France. In 1942, the cadets moved to Ribbesford House, near Bewdley and continued their training there until June 1944, when the young officers joined the invasion forces. About half were to lose their lives in battle. During their stay at Ribbesford, the cadets formed a mobile counter-attack column for an anti-invasion role in north Worcestershire. This proved to be a useful 'enemy' force in training exercises with the local Home Guard, when the boys from Ribbesford were known as the 'Fighting Free French'.

13/1 The Free French Cadets at Ribbesford House. After a short period in Wales, the Cadets de la France Libre *moved to House No 5 at Malvern College, in Worcestershire, and then to Ribbesford House, near Bewdley, in 1942. Here they trained as officer cadets for the return to France in 1944. (Photo: courtesy of Bewdley Museum)*

Dutch Forces

On the capitulation of Holland, Queen Wilhelmina, the Dutch government and units of the Dutch Army and Navy were able, with the help of the Royal Navy, to escape to Britain to carry on the fight. The Dutch Army in exile became the Royal Netherlands Brigade comprising: the 1st Battalion, The Royal Dutch Army; the 2nd Depot Battalion, RDA; a Light Aid Detachment; an Armoured Car Squadron; and the Royal Dutch Ordnance. The Brigade was accommodated until 1944 at Wrottesley Park, near Wolverhampton and, like the Czech forces, formed part of the region's anti-invasion defence force. The living quarters at Perton airfield were also used to accommodate some of the Dutch troops. After the liberation of parts of Holland in 1944, more young men were brought to Britain for equipping and training and the Wrottesley Park accommodation soon proved to be inadequate. A former American hospital camp at Wood Farm, Malvern was consequently taken over as a transit camp, where 3,000 Dutch troops were accommodated at one stage. At Wood Farm, troops from the front in North-West Europe would be demobilized and new recruits trained for the Far East campaign. An estimated total of 10,000 Dutch troops had passed through this transit camp by the time it was vacated in June 1946.

13/2 The Abbey Hotel, in Malvern, was requisitioned early in the Second World War and had a number of defence uses until returning to hotel use in 1946. Used initially by the Navy as a signals station, it was the headquarters of the Belgian Army in Britain during 1941 until occupied by the officers of RAF Malvern from May 1942 onwards. (Mick Wilks)

After the liberation of Holland over 200 hundred Dutch naval aircraft ground crew were trained at HMS Fledgling at Stoke on Trent (see chapter 12).

Belgian Forces

As elements of the 36th Independent Infantry Brigade, part of General Ironside's anti-invasion counter-attack force, moved out of Malvern in the spring of 1941, remnants of the Belgian Army that had earlier been brought off the beaches at Dunkirk moved in and established their headquarters in the Abbey Hotel. The Belgian troops were accommodated in a number of the larger houses in the town and in Hereford until the spring of 1942 when the scientists and staff of Telecommunications Research Establishment (TRE) and Air Defence Research and Development Establishment (ADRDE) came to Malvern and the Belgians moved to South Wales. In addition to the headquarters staff of the Belgian Army, the 2nd Battalion, Belgian Fusiliers, the Belgian Depot and Training Company and a Belgian Armoured Car Squadron were at Malvern, whilst the 3rd Battalion, Belgian Fusiliers and a Belgian Field Artillery Battery were billeted in Hereford.

Some of the Belgian pilots that had escaped from their country were trained at Rednal airfield in Shropshire before joining the RAF.

Czechoslovak Forces

Czech soldiers were also in the region, and a small number of handpicked men carried out one of the most audacious operations of the war. The Nazis had occupied the whole of Czechoslovakia in March 1939,

13/3 Now the Herefordshire County Record Office, these former militia barracks, off Harold Street in Hereford, were occupied by elements of the Belgian Army during 1941. (Mick Wilks)

the Czech President Beneš fleeing and forming a government-in-exile in London. Thousands of Czech servicemen also fled, fighting on the side of the French in the summer of 1940. The defeat of France led to Czechs joining the evacuation to Britain from French ports. Troops, landing at Liverpool, were sent to a tented camp in the grounds of Cholmondeley Castle Park, on the Cheshire/Shropshire border, these having been requisitioned by Western Command at the beginning of the war. Soon the troops were to be seen in the streets of Whitchurch, the officers being billeted in houses in the town. A school for Czech exiled children was established at nearby Hinton Hall, with Hinton Manor being leased by the Czech government-in-exile.

Everything did not run smoothly at the camp, however. Czechs who had served in the International Brigades in Spain objected to their officers and the politics of Beneš, and eventually 500 of these men were moved to the Prees Heath Internment Camp (see chapter 14) and then into the British Army's Pioneer Corps. The advent of autumn led to a move of the 3,200 men of the newly formed Czechoslovak Independent Brigade to a more permanent base in and around Leamington Spa. The local MP was the Foreign Secretary, Anthony Eden, but it is unclear if he played a part in the move. A headquarters was established at the now-demolished Harrington House in Newbold Terrace. The 1st Battalion was lodged in the grounds of Moreton Paddox whilst the 2nd Battalion was at Walton Hall, the Field Artillery Battery being at Moreton Hall. Umberslade

Park, Kineton and Butlers Marston accommodated the Reconnaissance Unit, the Machine Gun Company and a second battery respectively. NCOs and other ranks lived in wooden hutting, with the officers billeted in private houses. The men were kept busy at the Wedgenock firing range at Warwick, with field exercises on the Malvern Hills and Cannock Chase, together with the guarding of Wellesbourne Mountford airfield. In one Western Command exercise in North Shropshire codenamed 'Ariel', the keenness of the Czech and Dutch forces was noted; less complimentary views were expressed by the reviewing officer of the 'Tommies' who took part, it being felt that

13/4 Perhaps the most tangible reminder of the presence of the Czech Brigade in the Leamington area from 1940 onwards is this memorial fountain in the town's Jephson Gardens. (Bernard Lowry)

they lacked aggression. 'Ariel' was note-worthy, incidentally, as it involved one of the first instances of the use of British paratroops as the 'aggressor' force. They were then known by the code name '11th Special Air Service Force', in September 1941 being renamed the 1st Parachute Battalion. In April 1941 Churchill and his wife, together with US military and political dignitaries (the US had not yet entered the war) and Beneš, visited the Czechs at Moreton Paddox.

Beneš and the head of Czech Intelligence, Colonel Moravec, felt that their forces must carry out operations to revive Czech resistance in their home country. With SOE training and material assistance a number of teams of Czech servicemen were recruited from the men in Warwickshire and parachuted into Czechoslovakia from 1941 onwards. All operations failed with the exception of the most daring and important one: Operation Anthropoid, the assassination of the *Reichsprotektor* Heydrich in Prague in May 1942 by Sergeants Kubiš and Gabcik, who had both started at Cholmondeley Castle. All members of the team would lose their lives. Whilst striking a daring blow, the repercussions were terrible, leading to the final collapse of Czech resistance. The force remained as part of the Midland's anti-invasion reserve until the spring of 1942 when the entire Division moved to Ilminster in Dorset.

A number of officers and men of the Czech Air Force, some of whom had also recently fought with the French Air Force after escaping from Czechoslovakia, came to the Royal Air Force No 2 Technical Training School at Cosford, near Wolverhampton, between August and December 1940, where a Czech Depot had been established for testing and training personnel before being transferred to the RAF. Eventually four Czech squadrons would be formed within the RAF.

Polish Forces

Between late September 1940 and late May 1943 the Polish No 308 Squadron, operating Hawker Hurricane aircraft, was based at Baginton airfield to provide air defence for the Midlands; other Polish-manned Hurricanes had been at Tern Hill airfield in the summer of 1940. The Squadron was re-equipped with Spitfires in April 1943. Many of the Polish ground crew serving with the RAF were given technical training at the RAF schools at Cosford, Hednesford and Hereford, whilst in 1944 a Polish Service Training School for pilots converting to twin-engined aircraft established a special flight within No 577 Squadron, based at Castle Bromwich airfield, for both Poles and Czechs. Bramcote airfield, opened in the summer of 1940, trained Polish bomber crews until 1943.

A number of the redundant wartime camps in the Midlands were used by the Polish Resettlement Corps to accommodate returning Polish servicemen and their families after the Second World War. Those identified are the former American Hospital Camps at Kington and Foxley, Herefordshire, the former WAAF quarters at RAF Tilstock, Blackshaw Moor Army Camp near Leek and Wheaton Aston airfield, whilst the camp at Barons Cross, near Leominster became a Polish hospital.

Commonwealth Forces

A number of Canadian troops were accommodated at Foxley Manor in Herefordshire, the first to arrive being the 2nd Canadian Pioneer Battalion, which constructed a camp of wooden huts in the grounds of the manor. Other Canadian units followed until 1944.

The RAF No 23 Operational Training Unit was established at Pershore airfield, Worcestershire, in April 1941, to train Canadian aircrew for the Commonwealth squadrons of Bomber Command. No 81 OTU at Tilstock airfield, Shropshire, also trained Canadian and Australian aircrew, while No 27 OTU at Lichfield airfield, Staffordshire, trained Australians and New Zealanders. A significant number of graves of Canadian airmen in cemeteries in Worcester, Pershore and elsewhere bear witness to the sacrifice that Canada made in the air war.

Exotically, but for a short period only, an Indian Mule Company was billeted in Wormelow to the south of Hereford.

American Forces

The arrival of US troops from 1942 onwards in the country as part of Operation Bolero put further pressure on accommodation needs as the British Ministry of Works had to provide the majority of the accommodation for the incoming US forces, which, by D-Day, had reached one and a half million men. A new design introduced to meet these needs was the large Romney hut, generally used for storage (an early example was its use at a site near Wem in Shropshire by the US 83rd Ordnance Sub Depot). Another US depot (used post war by the RAOC) was the large camp at Moreton-on-Lugg, north of Hereford, provided with both Nissen and Romney huts, serviced by an extension of the local railway line. With large numbers of GIs and their equipment arriving at Liverpool Docks the Western Command area became extremely busy. Bridges such as the medieval one at Ludlow had to be given extra support to take heavier weights such as tank transporters.

In the build-up of American ground forces, the majority of the combat units of the 1st Army that were to be used in the initial landings in Normandy were accommodated in the south-western counties of Britain, with a headquarters in Bristol. The follow-up troops of General Patton's 3rd Army arrived in Britain in March 1944 and, with its headquarters at Peover Hall in Cheshire, were accommodated in the West Midlands region as far south as Herefordshire and Worcestershire in country houses and temporary tented camps referred to in chapter 11, as well as some of the newly built American hospital camps. A gradual movement southwards then followed as units were transported down to the south coast ports in stages and then to the landing beaches in Normandy. With the hospital camps emptied of combat troops, medical staff of the General and Station Hospitals moved in and prepared them to receive the casualties coming back from France and the subsequent campaigning in north-west Europe.

In the run up to D-Day the large number of US servicemen needing to be accommodated led to overcrowding in the

13/5 The former American forces jerrycan filling depot at Titton, near Stourport, is still largely complete and is now a small trading estate. It is a reminder of the massive logistical support system provided for American forces under the Operation Bolero scheme. (Mick Wilks)

camps and a more basic sewage disposal system being introduced to cope with this, often making use of latrine buckets (the GIs called them 'honey buckets') instead of built latrines. It also led to the occupation of semi-complete housing estates such as the Pheasey Farms Estate at Perry Barr, which became a sub-depot of the 10th Whittington Replacement Depot based at Whittington Barracks. GIs who had a roof over their heads could count themselves fortunate as many would have to live in tented camps supported by a basic infrastructure of roads, a water supply and pit latrines. Another example of US temporary accommodation was the camps established in the south of Shropshire to accommodate elements of the US 90th Infantry Division whose HQ was located in King Edward's School,

Birmingham. The segregation of black and white races within the US Army made the job of accommodation even more difficult. Each tented camp could accommodate 1,250 men berthed amongst 200 tents plus 20 Nissen huts and Ministry of Works concrete prefabricated huts for the messes, bathhouses, offices, kitchens etc. The camp locations were established in November 1943, but completion was often delayed due to shortages of materials. However, by April 1944 the south Shropshire camps were ready to receive US troops for training and by the beginning of May, 21,600 troops were based in Shropshire. Generals Patton and Bradley both visited the camps just before D-Day. The 90th Infantry Division, with an authorized strength of 14,000 men, suffered heavy casualties in the Normandy campaign,

13/6 The US Army 1st Base Post Office, Sutton Coldfield. Specially built to US requirements, the photograph shows the administration block with, to the far left, the loading area, mail being delivered by trains on lines which ran on the left of the picture. The site is still in use by the Royal Mail. (Bernard Lowry)

with 4,000 men being killed in action and 14,000 being wounded (including those called up to replace earlier losses).

Sutton Coldfield was the site of an important establishment (for US Army morale): the First Base Post Office. It handled all incoming post from the US for troops in Europe and North Africa and also sorted all outgoing mail to the US. The censoring of mail also took place here. It began life in July 1942 in a railway shed by the former LMS railway line in the town. A purpose-built building was soon erected (now listed Grade 2) supplemented by hutting as the FBPO expanded. A number of camps and barracks were established in the area to accommodate the 800 servicemen and women (plus numbers of local civilians) who worked there. An uncom-

pleted school in Holland Road, a Nissen hutted camp (Streetly Camp) in Sutton Park and a tented camp at Penns Lane were amongst the camps. With so many servicemen in the area it is not surprising to learn that a number of marriages with local women took place.

Another important US establishment in the area was Army Air Force Station 522 established in a requisitioned clothing factory in Beakes Road, Smethwick in the summer of 1943, closing in October 1945. The station was used to store, supply and repair radar and radio equipment for US bases in the UK. After D-Day a branch of the station was established on the Continent, it being a branch of the large Base Air Depot at Burtonwood in Lancashire. Recreation facilities for this and other US facilities were provided by the American Red Cross Club in New Street, Birmingham.

At Yarnfield near Stone in Staffordshire, occupying hostels built for the Swynnerton ordnance factory, were the US Army Air Force Stations 518, 509 and 594 accommodating freshly-trained pilots awaiting transfer to units. The hostels had been named 'Beatty', Duncan' and 'Howard', although the latter also appears to have been given the American name of 'Jefferson'.

The Americans centred their Services of Supply in Cheltenham, with a series of large, above ground storage depots generally in the area to the south of the town through Gloucestershire, Wiltshire and Somerset, but one was located in Honeybourne in Worcestershire, and another on the border of Worcestershire and Gloucestershire at Ashchurch, near Tewkesbury. The former was abandoned by the Americans at the end of the war. They left many of their stores there and set off one of the biggest black market scandals of post-war Britain. Some of the site has been redeveloped to become Long Lartin Prison, but many of the Romney storage huts remain. Ashchurch was re-occupied by the British Army at the end of the war and is still used by the Army Logistical Corps for the storage of military equipment.

As noted in chapter 10 Atcham airfield was one of the first British airfields to be handed over to the American 8th Air Force as a Combat Crew Replacement Centre. Here newly arrived fighter pilots would become accustomed to flying in British weather before being posted to their combat units. With the build-up of the 9th Air Force, Atcham became the theatre training centre for its replacement pilots too. Part of Wolverley Camp, near Kidderminster, was temporarily used as a radio training school for air force personnel and called USAAF Station 509, Radio Training School.

PRISONERS OF WAR CAMPS 14

The battles of the First World War resulted in the capture of many German and Austrian soldiers, particularly towards the end when German positions were being overrun. Prisoners of War camps were set up throughout the United Kingdom and also in the dominions and the then colonies. In the West Midlands there were about 60 such camps with the majority being located in the more rural areas. This is not surprising as PoWs were often used as farm labourers. The treatment of such prisoners had been codified in the 1907 Hague Convention which set out that they could be used in non-military work, which agriculture was judged to be.

During the 1914-19 period, the camps were either in requisitioned buildings or tents. It is not known how many of each

there were. The official list contains the names of a few of the requisitioned buildings but the details of some other buildings are known from a variety of local sources. Many of these buildings still exist, often being requisitioned again in the Second World War, including Park Hall in Shropshire, Somerford Hall and Wrottesley Hall in Staffordshire, and Hillhampton House and Rochford House in Worcestershire. Of course, nothing remains of the tented camps although in a few cases their approximate location is known.

The treatment of prisoners was reviewed after the First World War and expanded provisions were set out in the Geneva Convention of 1929. Its provisions provided for the protection of

14/1 Remains of First World War PoW camp at Shelsley Walsh, Worcestershire. (Colin Jones)

14/2 *Somerford Hall and grounds, Breewood, Staffordshire. Site of First World War PoW camp. (Colin Jones)*

military personnel from their capture to their release. Upon capture military personnel had only to give their name, rank and service number. Captured military personnel were *not* to be tortured. During the Second World War the USA and the UK (including the Dominions) in the main did follow the provisions of the Geneva Convention, but the same cannot be said of the Germans, the Japanese or the Russians. (It should be noted that Japan and the Soviet Union were not signatories of the Geneva Convention; the Germans used this as an excuse for their mistreatment of Russian PoWs.) The Geneva Convention was revised in 1949 to include non-combatants.

By the end of the Second World War there were over half a million German and Italian PoWs in many camps throughout the UK. An English Heritage report lists about 46 in the West Midlands, but this is probably an under-estimate as we know of

camps not on the list, unless these were sub-camps of those listed.

Again, large buildings were requisitioned for use as camps although these mainly held officers who, under the terms of the Geneva Convention, were not required to work. Whilst initially other camps may have been tented they were soon replaced by more permanent buildings. Often the prisoners themselves were used in constructing the buildings that were to house them; presumably living temporarily in tents encouraged the prisoners to waste no time in constructing the permanent buildings. In some cases towards the end of the war PoW camps were located in what had previously been US and UK military camps, which had become empty after the invasion of Europe. An example of the different housing of officers and other ranks is a camp near Droitwich, Worcestershire, where the officers were housed in Chateau Impney (previously a country house and now a hotel) whilst other ranks were in a hutted camp at Hampton Lovett. Other large buildings requisitioned for use as PoW camps included Teddesley and Loxley Halls (Staffs), Adderley Hall and Davenport House (Shrops), Merevale Hall (Warwicks) and Perdiswell Hall (Worcs).

As in the First World War many prisoners worked on farms during and after the war although some were used for clearing bomb sites and, after the end of the war, clearing coastal defences and in other similar work. In the early years of the war most were Italians captured in North Africa; the few Germans were either seamen or air crew. The position of Italian PoWs became slightly anomalous after 1943 when Italy surrendered to the Allies, for the northern part of Italy was then occupied by the Germans and so it was not possible to repatriate PoWs. Also, the Italians had become an important part of the UK's agricultural workforce who would not be easy to replace. The Italians were told they would remain prisoners, but as their work was helping to

bring forward the defeat of Germany their conditions were eased and they could also be employed on war work. Most continued working on the land till the end of the war, with many living on the farms where they worked or in hostels. This freed up the camps for the increasing number of Germans captured after the invasion of France in 1944. It should be pointed out that farmers had to pay the government for their use of PoWs and that the prisoners did receive some small recompense for the work they did. This was usually in the form of tokens that could be spent in the camp shop. The Italians were paid more generously from 1944 onwards and were allowed to change part of their earnings into currency for sending home.

Whilst most Italian PoWs were employed in agriculture this was not the case with German prisoners. These latter were categorised and only those who were classified as definitely non-Nazi were allowed to be employed outside the camps. Ardent Nazis were usually kept in separate camps or separate parts of camps as they

14/3 St Martins, Shropshire. A Second World War PoW camp now in use as an industrial estate. (Bernard Lowry)

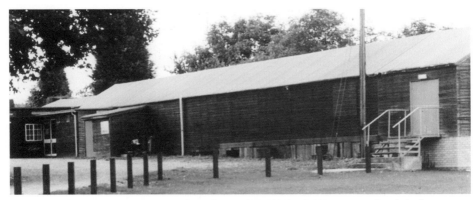

14/4 The last remaining hut of the Second World War PoW camp at South Littleton, Worcestershire. (Colin Jones)

often victimised their less politically motivated brethren: there were even instances of the murder of fellow prisoners. When repatriation started it was the less politically motivated who were sent home first. By the end of 1948 repatriation had ended, with most prisoners having returned home. Those who stayed did so voluntarily either to work on the land or because they had married locals.

Examples of Second World War PoW camps can still be seen near Oswestry and near Gobowen (both Shropshire – for exact locations see gazetteer). In most other cases very little is left, apart from the remains of approach roads, water towers and the concrete hut bases, with the latter sometimes being used for the standings of caravans. Some of the requisitioned buildings also still remain, examples being Loxley Hall (Staffs) and Chateau Impney (Worcs).

Internment

In both world wars there was internment of enemy aliens, with just under 30,000 being interned in each war and with the main internment centre being on the Isle of Man, although in the Second World War some were sent to Australia or Canada. Prior to going to the Isle of Man or the dominions enemy aliens were housed in temporary camps which were often not much more than collections of tents (but then they only existed from the summer of 1940 until that October). Two temporary Second World War internment camps in the West Midlands were at Prees Heath (Shrops) and Sutton Coldfield, both being tented. Nothing remains of either camp. Prees Heath camp remains well known as two members of what became the Amadeus String Quartet met there. They met a third future member at the Isle of Man internment camp, but did not meet the fourth till after the war.

TREATING THE CASUALTIES

15

The sight of rows of headstones in military cemeteries is one of the most poignant reminders that war inevitably results in casualties. Although France and Flanders provide the most dramatic of such cemeteries, it is not necessary to go there to see rows of Commonwealth War Graves Commission headstones (CWGC); they exist in the Midlands. On Cannock Chase is a CWGC cemetery and also a German war grave cemetery. But military personnel were not the only casualties of war and in the Second World War particularly, civilians became very much part of the 'front line' during the night raids by the Luftwaffe. In many cases these civilian casualties were so mutilated by bomb blast that it was impossible to identify them, or they simply disappeared, just as so many soldiers had done on the Western Front in the First World War. The raid on Coventry, on 14 November 1940, was just one example where a mass grave was used to inter the remains of those civilians that could be found, with a memorial erected in the memory of all of those lost. It is a sad fact that the death toll of civilians in Britain as a result of enemy bombing exceeded that of our military forces until 1942, almost half of them being in London. But what of those military personnel and civilians who were injured in the two main conflicts of the twentieth century? The Midlands would provide treatment

and care for many of them and it is with this aspect of 'defence' that this chapter is largely concerned.

After the lamentable treatment of sick and injured soldiers in the Crimean War and again in the South African War at the beginning of the twentieth century, when many died of wounds or sickness that could have been prevented with proper care, a number of arrangements were made to help avoid a repetition in any future wars. An independent Royal Army Medical Corps had already been formed in 1898, but recognition by the War Office that women generally provided more efficient care for casualties than male orderlies resulted in the formation of the Queen Alexandra's Imperial Military Nursing Service (QAIMNS) in 1902. This was supplemented in 1908 by the QAIMNS Reserve and by the Territorial Army Nursing Service and, before the First World War, by the formation of the First Aid Nursing Yeomanry (FANY) as a military ambulance service. A significant contribution to the treatment of wartime casualties was also provided by other voluntary organizations, principally the Red Cross Society and the Order of St John, both of which would come under military control in wartime, when they would undertake a variety of duties.

Prior to the First World War, a War Office instruction to every county

15/1 This image of a Cross of Sacrifice and row upon row of Commonwealth War Graves Commission headstones might suggest a scene from the Western Front, but this cemetery can be found on Cannock Chase, in Staffordshire. There is also a large German forces cemetery close by. (Bernard Lowry)

Territorial Association required that it should obtain the assistance of Voluntary Aid Detachments (VAD) to supplement the military nursing and ambulance services at the outbreak of war. The enrolment of the VADs was undertaken by the county branches of the Red Cross Society and by the St John Ambulance Association. A Joint War Committee, activated in both World Wars, would co-ordinate their efforts. With the unprecedented numbers of civilian casualties in the Second World War, the Red Cross also became part of the Civil Nursing Reserve providing help in civilian hospitals.

In both World Wars army casualties would receive first aid from medical staff of the Royal Army Medical Corps and, depending on the severity of the injuries, a battlefield casualty would then progress through a regimental aid post (RAP) to an advanced dressing station, a casualty clearing station and then to a base or field hospital. For those combatants too badly injured or ill to be treated abroad, transport was provided by boat and specially equipped trains to hospitals throughout Britain. In the Second World War, aircraft would also be used to transfer casualties to Britain and a number of airfields or grassed landing strips were employed for this purpose (see chapter 10). After a further period of hospital care and convalescence, and depending on the level of recovery, a casualty might be returned to his unit, posted to a position involving lighter duties, or discharged from all duties with a pension.

The nineteenth-century regimental depots at Whittington Barracks near Lichfield, Budbrooke Barracks at Warwick, and Norton Barracks at Worcester, were provided with small hospitals for the treatment of troops under their control, while in the Second World War the larger airfields and the temporary naval stations would each have a sick quarters for the treatment of sick or injured airmen and sailors. While these might be adequate for peacetime military purposes or less urgent cases, in wartime the government would earmark bed spaces in existing civilian hospitals, as well as requisitioning schools and other educational establishments, town halls and hotels for the treatment or convalescence of military casualties, with a number of voluntary organizations providing the extra nursing and ambulance capacity required. The owners of many large country houses and local authorities would also make a significant contribution to the treatment of casualties in both World Wars by offering the use of their properties to the government as temporary hospitals, although the demand for such temporary facilities was greatest in the first conflict when over 130 such properties in the West Midlands were used.

A good example of earmarking and then occupation of civilian property for

additional bed spaces in wartime was the 1st Southern General Hospital at Edgbaston, which occupied a number of buildings at the University of Birmingham, including University Hall. The buildings had been earmarked prior to the First World War and were occupied and adapted to become a military hospital with 520 bed spaces on 4 August 1914, the day that war was declared. The first convoy of casualties was received on 1 September, including some Belgian troops. By the end of the year the hospital was expanded to

15/2 University Hall, at Birmingham University, Edgbaston, formed the basis of the 1st Southern Military Hospital during the First World War. Before the war was over more university buildings and other large houses in the region would be taken over as temporary hospitals to cope with the large numbers of casualties. (Photo: Colin Jones)

15/3 One of a number of emergency hospitals built in the Midlands in anticipation of large civilian casualties caused by bombing, this one at Evesham survives as the town's General Hospital. It was utilised during the war by the RAF to treat the sick and injured airmen and aircrew from the training establishments in the area. (Mick Wilks)

provide 800 beds and steps were taken to establish further auxiliary hospitals in the vicinity. The first of these was the Poor Law Infirmary in the Dudley Road, Birmingham, which was opened in May 1915. Twenty-three auxiliary hospitals were to be affiliated to the 1st Southern General Hospital, providing a total of over 7,000 bed spaces by the time of demobilization in the spring of 1920. Some were located as far away as Stourbridge, Coventry, Rugby, Warwick, Leamington, Stratford and Shipston-on-Stour. Some of the bed spaces were provided in tents set up in the grounds of the university and the other properties.

With the Army Council predicting a substantial increase in casualties, the Asylum War Hospitals scheme was instituted for the whole country in January 1915, under which those asylums with modern buildings would become surgical

and medical hospitals. Asylums at Rubery, which became the 1st Birmingham War Hospital, and Hollymoor, that became the 2nd Birmingham War Hospital, were incorporated into the scheme, as were asylums at Winson Green in Birmingham; Stafford, Burntwood and Cheddleton in Staffordshire; Salop County Asylum at Shelton; Warwick County Asylum at Hatton; and Powick and Barnsley Hall Asylums in Worcestershire.

Some of the great houses of the Midlands used as auxiliary hospitals during the First World War were Hawkestone Park, Attingham Park, Hodnet Hall and Stokesay Court in Shropshire; Hartlebury Castle, Rhydd Court at Hanley Castle, and The Grange at Halesowen in Worcestershire; and Maxstoke Castle and Harborne Hall in Warwickshire.

Before the Second World War civilian hospitals were provided by either local authorities or voluntary organizations, with the latter relying on charity and private donations for their running costs. In the period immediately before the Second World War, the government predicted massive civilian casualties as a result of heavy aerial bombing, so an Emergency Hospital Service was established to co-ordinate the treatment of casualties in likely danger areas. Surveys suggested that there would be a serious shortage of bed spaces and that the standard of treatment available under the two systems of hospital provision then running, private and public, would vary considerably. Consequently a number of emergency hospitals were constructed, annexed to existing hospitals, using temporary hutting to provide many new bed spaces and operating theatres, and a National Blood Transfusion Service was established. Under the Emergency Hospital Service, free treatment would be given to both civilian and military war casualties, but the scheme did not include the sick and elderly. By 1942 the Medical Planning Commission was proposing a unified, centrally planned public medical service and following the Beveridge Report of 1944, the National Health Service was established in the post-war era. It is interesting to reflect that, in the current absence of any permanent military hospi-tals in Britain, an NHS hospital at Selly Oak in the Midlands is presently the focus for the treatment of all seriously injured mili-tary casualties.

During the Second World War the number of private properties requisi-tioned for hospital use was much smaller than in the previous conflict, 50 being used or earmarked in the West Midlands. Again, some of the great country houses or parks were involved, such as Shugborough Hall in Staffordshire; Berrington Hall, near Leominster, in Herefordshire; Stoneleigh Abbey and Ragley Hall in Warwickshire; and Himley Hall in Dudley. The charity providing rehabilitation for blinded servicemen, St Dunstan's, used a number of properties in the Church Stretton area for a time during the Second World War including what is now the Longmynd Hotel.

The terrible scourge of tuberculosis, only defeated by the availability of drugs after the Second World War, was not just a deadly killer of civilians. Prisoners of war, sailors in cramped conditions on ships, especially submarines, and servicemen in unhealthy parts of the world caught TB as it was then called. The Cheshire Joint Sanatorium at Loggerheads in Staffordshire treated many servicemen, the doctor in charge, Peter Edwards, being a Major in a local Home Guard unit.

Most of the temporary hutted wartime emergency hospitals have now been cleared away but some saw continued service in the National Health Service for many years, such as the Ronkswood Hospital in Worcester. Part of one still remains at Evesham and another at Shrewsbury (Copthorne), where the temporary brick and asbestos structures are still in hospital use.

The arrival of Americans in Britain, from 1942 onwards, to participate in the bombing campaign against the Axis powers and as part of the build-up of forces for the invasion of France in 1944, led to a further and substantial demand

15/4 Now used as a training establishment, some of the ward buildings of the former American 307th Station Hospital can still be seen at Stoneleigh, in Warwickshire, to the east of the Royal Agricultural Showground. (Steve Carvell)

for hospital capacity: 90,000 additional bed spaces were calculated as being required by April 1944. Some British hospitals were transferred to the Americans and some suitable country houses were made available, but the majority of that capacity would come from the construction of new facilities. The relatively tranquil rural areas in the West Midlands were chosen to locate the bulk of the new American hospitals, with Worcestershire and Herefordshire accommodating a particularly large concentration, administered from the 12th Medical Hospital Centre in Malvern. There was a smaller scatter of facilities in the northern part of the region, administered from Whitchurch. Many of these new hospital camps were designed to have a dual purpose: accommodation for troops moving through the area during the build-up to the D-Day landings (see chapter 13) and then use as general hospitals after D-Day.

Most of the American hospitals were built during 1943 by British contractors to American designs and specifications, one of the first to be commissioned being located at Wolverley, north of Kidderminster. After D-Day, the transport of American casualties from the battlefields would normally be by hospital boat and then train, although aircraft were used, commonly the Douglas C47 Dakota, to bring in cases requiring particularly urgent treatment, and a number of West Midlands airfields were used for this purpose. The hospital trains were staffed by Americans and would bring the patients to railway stations convenient to the clusters of hospitals. During the journey from the south coast ports by these trains, an assessment would be made of the treatment required by each patient so that, on arrival at the terminal station, ambulances would be detailed to take the men to the appropriate specialist hospitals, including those treating psychiatric problems. One station, at Malvern Wells in Worcestershire, was to have a special siding constructed to accommodate American hospital trains whilst the patients were transferred to ambulances; there were probably other examples.

After treatment at one of the specialist hospitals, casualties would be returned to the USA and discharged if their injuries resulted in permanent disability, or sent to convalescent hospitals before returning to duties. In the Midlands, convalescent hospitals were provided at Stoneleigh Abbey and Packington Hall, Warwickshire, and at Bromsgrove in Worcestershire.

The Americans provided opportunities for rest and recuperation (R&R) and a number of large houses and hotels were requisitioned for men to take a week's leave from combat duties. The Star Hotel (now Whitehouse Hotel) in Worcester, for example, was requisitioned for this purpose, and Spetchley Court was used by American aircrew needing a rest from combat flying, being known as the 'Flak Shack'. Every town would have its 'Donut Dugout' and a Red Cross Club for American servicemen to meet and relax after duty. These were run by members of the American Red Cross, which also provided support to both patients and staff at the hospitals.

The Americans vacated the hospitals soon after the war, after which the camps were used for a variety of purposes: some would be used by British forces returning

*15/5 Among the more substantial remnants of the American presence in the Midlands are the emergency water supply towers provided for their hospitals, such as this massive twin tower at Blackmore, near Malvern.
(Mick Wilks)*

from overseas as barracks; others were used as PoW camps or for displaced persons, including the Polish Resettlement Corps; whilst a few would be retained as hospitals for civilian use. Most have now been cleared of buildings although remnants remain in the Midlands as small trading estates, or are used for agricultural purposes. Enduring remains of the American hospitals are the massive brick-built emergency water supply tanks and the concrete approach roads.

SITE GAZETTEER

NOTES

1. This is a list of examples that were surviving when this book was written (summer, 2007). It is not a complete inventory and, in the main, only lists sites that can be seen from roads or other public rights of way.

2. Where national grid references are quoted they are usually 6-figure and thus only approximate. Where known 8-figure references are quoted.

3. As stated in the Introduction, care should be taken when visiting sites as they can be dangerous after 60+ years of neglect. Where the site is on private land, permission of the landowner should be obtained.

Chapter I

Munitions
ROF Rotherwas, Holme Lacy Road, Hereford. Some remains can be seen in the industrial estate on the north and south sides of the road. Further along (ie. to the east) is what was the administrative block of the ROF. SO 535 378.

ROF, Blackpole Road, Worcester. This is now an industrial estate but some of the original buildings can still be seen. SO 866 579.

ROF Swynnerton. Parts of the site can be seen from public footpath leading from Cotes to the Swynnerton – Coldmeece Road. SJ 846 345.

ROF Summerfield, A449, nr Kidderminster. Some Second World War buildings can be seen from the A449. SO 840 735.

ROF Featherstone, near Wolverhampton. A small part of the site can be seen from Brookhouse Lane which runs alongside the M54. SJ 925 050.

Sentinel Works, Whitchurch Road, Shrewsbury. Factory made shell casings in Second World War, also Bren Gun Carriers. SJ 504 148.

Note: Aerial views of some of these ROFs (including Swynnerton) can be seen on the internet sites www.maps.live.com and www.192.com.

Aircraft (including parts)
Boulton Paul, Pendeford, Wolverhampton. The original factory, now owned by Smiths Aerospace, is on the Wobaston Road next to the Shropshire Union Canal. SO 889 033.

Morris Motors, Castle Bromwich, Birmingham. Complex now owned by Jaguar. Second World War buildings can be seen from Heartlands Spine Road. SP 137 907.

Peaton. The remains of the factory can still be seen in a field NW of Peaton on the minor road from Diddlebury to Tugford. SO 528 851.

Rolls Royce (now Leoni Wiring Systems), Lower Milehouse Lane, Newcastle-under-Lyme. The factory was involved in jet engine development during the Second World War. SJ 838 477.

Heenan & Froude, Shrub Hill Road, Worcester. The factory, which produced aircraft engine parts during the Second World War, can be seen on both sides of the road. SO 856 552.

Midland Red, Whitchurch Road, Shrewsbury. Part of the then Midland Red (now Arriva) bus garage was used in the Second World War to make aircraft parts. SJ 499 138.

Other War Materials
Petrol Depot, Ripple, near Upton-on-Severn. Site can be seen from public footpaths near to the River Severn. SO 864 395.

Petrol Depot, Worcester Road, Titton, near Stourport. Site shown as sewage works on Ordnance Survey maps. SO 823 700.

Pumping Station (for PLUTO), near Fordhall Farm, A53, near Market Drayton. The buildings can be seen from the track leading to the farm. SJ 649 330.

Petrol Can Filling Depot, A4025, Titton, near Stourport. Second World War huts can be seen on north side of road. SO 828 698.

The Civil Defence Camouflage Directorate. In the Second World War this was based at the Regent Hotel, The Parade, Leamington Spa. SP 317 658.

Explosives Storage
Nesscliffe, Shropshire (former Central Ammunition Depot). Camp buildings visible from the village of Wilcott. Many of the large ammunition magazines, together with the traces of the railway spurs that supplied them, are visible from lanes and public footpaths paths in the area between Shrawardine and Knockin. SJ 375 185.

Fauld, Staffordshire (explosion crater). Accessible by public footpaths running east from Hanbury village. SK 183 278.

Fauld, Staffordshire. Buildings associated with the former RAF bomb store are visible from the lane running from Tutbury to Coton in the Clay. SK 182 286.

Chapter 2

Birmingham University, Edgbaston, Birmingham. SP 048 835.

Main school building, Malvern College. Can be seen from College Road, Malvern. SO 777 452.

The Monastery, Malvern College. Can be seen from College Road, Malvern. SO 777 454.

Preston Science Laboratory. Can be seen from Thirlstane Road, Malvern. SO 777 449.

The TRE Engineering Unit. Can be seen from Geraldine Road, Malvern. SO 787 452.

The TRE Hostel communal building. Can be seen from Geraldine Road, Malvern. SO 790 451.

The Qinetiq Site (formerly the post-war TRE and RRE site), St Andrew's Road, Malvern. Can be seen from nearby roads. SO 785 447.

TRE radio listening post. Can be seen from the nearby lane at Guarlford, Worcs. SO 809 450.

Earl's Croome Court. Can be seen from nearby road at Earl's Croome, Worcs. SO 869 420.

ADRDE Trials Field. Can be seen from the nearby lane at Earl's Croome, Worcs. SO 873 427.

Defford Airfield, Worcestershire. Surviving T2 hangar, but re-clad, can be seen from nearby road. SO 893 434.

Defford Airfield Sick Quarters Site. Can be visited at Croome Park (National Trust), Worcs. SO 887 452.

Pershore Airfield. Control tower and hangars can be seen from public road, near Throckmorton, Worcs. SO 972 497.

Operational Building, TRE's Experimental GCI Radar Site, Sledge Green, Worcs. Can be seen from nearby lane. SO 806 338.

Chapter 3

Hostels
Bishops Wood Women's Timber Corps Hostel. On W edge of the wood by Moss Lane Farm, Staffordshire. SJ 744 309.

Training colleges for the Land Army
Studley Horticultural and Agricultural College for Women (former). 1 mile NE of the village of Studley, Warwks. SP 088 641.

Harper Adams Agricultural College (now University College). On N edge of the village of Edgmond, Shrops. SJ 713 204.

Pershore Agricultural College, ('Avonbank'). Between Pershore and the village of Wick, Worcs, on the B4084. SO 957 447.

Food
Buffer Depot, Albany Terrace, Worcester. The Second World War food store can still be seen opposite the end of York Place next to the church. SO 842 557.

Grain Silo, Audley Avenue, Newport, Shrops. A Second World War depot. SJ 7544 1852.

Cold Store, Harlescott Lane, Shrewsbury. Another Second World War depot. SJ 510 159.

Buffer Depot, A34 at Walton, Stone, Staffs. Yet another Second World War depot. SJ 9038 3272.

British Restaurant, Town Hall, Market Place, Evesham. The hall is in Market Place alongside Vine Street. SP 0369 4378.

Chapter 4

BBC, Wood Norton, Evesham. The site is off the A44. The main building is now a hotel and thus open to the public. Visitors can see some of the buildings some of which remain in use by the BBC. SP 017 472.

BBC Transmitters, Wychbold, Bromsgrove. The aerials can be seen from the A38 and the M5. SO 927 665.

BBC Transmitters, Woofferton, Ludlow. SO 510 682. The site is on the B4362 road but the aerials can also be seen from the minor road from the A49 to Richards Castle.

BT Radio Station, near Hillmorton, Rugby. Very little remains as the last aerials were dismantled in 2007. However the site can be seen from the A5. SP 554 746.

'Y' Service
The Old Rectory, Whitchurch, Shrops. Former Second World War and Cold War Foreign Office wireless intercept station. Visible from London Road/Claypit Street area. SJ 542 421.

Woodhead Hall, Staffs. RAF Cheadle wireless intercept station. Visible from minor road running south from Kingsley Holt. SK 025 447.

Newbold Revel, Stretton-under-Fosse, Warwickshire. RAF wireless intercept training school (now used by Prison Service as training school). Visible from the public bridleway running from Stretton under Fosse, and passing through the park. SP 455 808.

Chapter 5

Madresfield Court (Royal Family), near Malvern. Grounds occasionally opened to the public (otherwise the court cannot be seen). SO 808 475.

Pitchford Hall (Royal Family), near Shrewsbury. Not open to the public but can be seen from nearby road. SJ 528 042.

Bevere Manor (Government Ministers), near Worcester. Not open to the public but can be glimpsed from nearby road. SO 842 594.

Hindlip Hall (Government Ministers), Fernhill Heath, near Worcester (now West Mercia Police HQ). Not open to public but can be seen from nearby lanes and the A38. SO 881 586.

Spetchley Court (Winston Churchill), near Worcester. Grounds open in the summer from where the house can be seen. Back of house can clearly be seen from a public footpath which goes through the grounds. SO 896 538.

Malvern College (Admiralty and Cabinet meetings), Great Malvern. Can be seen from College Road. SO 779 452.

The Abbey Hotel (the first Admiralty Signals Station), Priory Road, Great Malvern. SO 776 458.

The Civil Service Social Club (later purpose-built Admiralty Signals Station), Spring Lane, off Pickersleigh Avenue, Malvern Link. SO 788 475.

The Royal Shakespeare Theatre (for full Government sittings), Stratford upon Avon. SP 203 547.

Bromsgrove School (Foreign Office), Worcester Road, Bromsgrove. Can be seen from nearby roads. SO 948 692.

Kings School (Air Ministry), Worcester. Can be seen from College Green. SO 850 544.

TOBs (Air Ministry), Whittington Road, Worcester. Can be seen during working hours. SO 873 537.

TOBs (Air Ministry), Oldbury Road, St John's, Worcester. Can be seen within the University of Worcester campus. SO 834 556.

TOBs (Admiralty and HMS Duke), off St Andrew's Road, Malvern. Now the Qinetiq site and few are left, but can be seen from nearby roads. SO 785 447.

Overbury Court (The Bank of England), Overbury, Worcestershire. The grounds are occasionally open to the public but the house can be seen from the road. SO 957 375.

Eastington Hall (The Tate Gallery), near Longdon, Worcestershire. Not open to the public but can be seen from nearby lane. SO 831 381.

Hellens (also used as temporary store for Tate Gallery paintings), Much Marcle, Herefordshire. Open to the public. SO 661 332.

The former chapel (now a mosque) of the **Hillborough Workhouse** (an emergency Fighter Control Room established by the Air Ministry), Tallow Hill, Worcester. Can be seen from adjoining roads. SO 857 551.

Trentham Gardens (Central Clearing Bank), near Stoke on Trent, Staffordshire. House has gone but grounds remain. SJ 860 410.

For **BBC Wychbold and BBC Wood Norton** see the Gazetteer for chapter 4.

Chapter 6

Defence Forces Headquarters
III Corps Headquarters, Whitchurch Rectory, Shropshire. Can be seen from London Road. SJ 542 421.

2nd London Division Headquarters, Whitney Court, Herefordshire. Collapsed tunnel entrances can still be seen from a public footpath below the court. SO 270 477.

No 23 Infantry Training Centre, Norton Barracks, Worcester. The Keep is now in residential use but adjoins Crookbarrow Road. SO 869 518.

Western Command Stop Line
The stop lines in the Midlands display the most significant collection of surviving defence structures and most can be seen from adjoining rights of way or roads.

The Avon Stop Line
Spigot Mortar pedestal, **Bredon**, Worcs. Located at junction of the B 4080 and B 4079 roads. SO 927 368.
Stent pillbox and Spigot Mortar pedestals, **Eckington Bridge**, Worcs. SO 922 423.

Anti-tank cylinders, Spigot Mortar pedestal, infantry trenches and a modified Hotchkiss 6 pdr emplacement, **Pershore Bridges** Picnic Place, Worcs. SO 952 451.
FW3/24 type pillbox, anti-tank cylinders, road block sockets in the ramp to the ford and Spigot Mortar pedestal, Fish and Anchor Ford, **Offenham**, Worcs. SP 065 471.
Two octagonal concrete blocks, at **Leafield Bridge**, near Warwick. SP 280 631.

The Severn Stop Line
Aircraft landing obstacles (trenches), **Tewkesbury Ham**. SO 885 325.
Aircraft landing obstacles (trenches), **Upton upon Severn Ham**. SO 860 400.
Anti-tank cylinders, Hanley Road, **Upton upon Severn**. SO 850 408.
Loop-holed building, **Diglis Weir, Worcester**. Can be seen from public footpath on the opposite west bank of the river. SO 847 534.
Hotchkiss 6 pdr emplacement, **Holt Fleet Bridge**, Worcs. SO 825 634.
Anti-tank cylinders, **Stourport on Severn** Fun Fair, Worcs. SO 808 711.
Aircraft landing obstacle (anchor stanchion for cable), **Stourport** riverside footpath. SO 812 708.
Anti-tank cylinders at Finger Post, **Far Forest**, Worcs. SO 737 739.
Anti-tank cylinders adjoining Richmond Road, **Bewdley**, Worcs. SO 783 759.
Spigot Mortar pedestal, adjoining the road bridge over the Severn, Low Town, **Bridgnorth**, Shrops. SO 718 932.
Road block sockets in rock cutting for an estate road in **Apley Park**, near Bridgnorth, Shrops. SJ 710 983.
FW3/24 type pillbox, Apley Forge, **Apley Park**, near Bridgnorth, Shrops. SO 707 983.
Two FW3/22 type pillboxes, **Cressage Bridge**, Shrops. SJ 594 046 and SJ 595 044.

The Teme Stop Line

Anti-tank cylinders, **Hipplecote**, near Ankerdine Hill, Worcs. SO 743 576.

Anti-tank cylinders, alongside the B4204, at Hillend, near **Martley**, Worcs. SO 745 605.

Home Guard ammunition store, **New Mill Bridge**, near Shelsley Beauchamp, Worcs. SO 728 624.

Hybrid design pillbox, **Stanford on Teme Bridge**, Worcs. SO 715 658.

Anti-tank cylinders, Long Bank, **Eastham**, Worcs. SO 671 675.

The abutments of a canal aqueduct, destroyed in 1940, can be seen near footpath at **Little Hereford**, Herefs. SO 538 687.

The Wye Stop Line

Variant of FW3/24 type pillbox, **Huntsham Bridge**, near Goodrich, Herefs. SO 567 182.

Loopholed mill, **Mordiford**, Herefs. SO 572 373.

Norcon pillbox, **Bridge Sollers**, Herefs. SO 413 426.

The Trent, Coventry and Oxford Canals Stop Line

FW3/26 type pillbox at **Wolseley Bridge**, near Colwich (by side of A513). SK 019 203.

FW3/24 type pillboxes at **Yoxall**, Staffs. Visible from A515 south of Yoxall. SK 113 176 and SK 131 181.

Pillbox at **Fradley Bridge**, Staffs., on the Coventry Canal. SK 153 131.

FW3/24 type pillbox, on W bank of the River Tame, **Elford**, Staffs. SK 184 104.

Two FW3/24 type pillboxes, **Walton on Trent**, Derbys. Visible from road into village. SK 205 167 and SK 208 179.

Two FW3/24 type pillboxes, near **Walton Bridge**. SK 212 180 and SK 213 183.

FW3/24 type pillbox, **Croxall**, Staffs. Visible from river bridge. SK 186 138.

FW3/24 type pillbox. W side of the river, **Wychnor**, Staffs. SK 181 161.

FW3/24 type pillbox at National Memorial Arboretum, **Alrewas**, Staffs, by the River Tame. SK 189 148.

FW3/24 type pillbox, **Hopwas**, Staffs. By canal N of Hopwas. SK 179 053.

FW3/24 type pillbox, Hints Road, **Hopwas**. In the front garden of a house. SK 181 050.

FW3/24 type pillbox, S of **Hopwas**. Visible from lane. SK 183 046.

FW3/24 type pillbox, **Tamworth**. Accessible from public footpath by riverside. SK 204 037. This pillbox would have contributed to the anti-tank island defences.

Converted dovecote defence post, **Alvecote Priory**, near Tamworth. SK 251 043.

FW3/23 type pillbox, **Curdworth**, Warwks. SK 187 930.

Anti-tank pimples, **Newbold on Avon**, NW of Rugby. SP 488 773.

The Trent, Tame, Dove and Churnet Stop Line

FW3/24 type pillbox, **Marchington**, Staffs. Visible from footpath S of Sudbury. SK 151 316.

FW3/24 type pillbox, **Fauld**, near Tutbury, Staffs. Visible from lane. SK 190 290.

FW3/24 type pillbox, on the River Dove, N of **Uttoxeter**. Visible from footpath. SK 100 376.

FW3/24 type pillboxes. Visible from footpath on the **River Dove**. SK 105 345 and SK 106 344.

FW3/24 type pillboxes. Two miles E of Uttoxeter. Visible from footpaths from **Doveridge** to the river. SK 111 339 and SK 113 334.

FW3/24 type pillbox. Near Eaton Dovedale Farm, **Rocester**, Staffs. SK 010 376.

FW3/24 type pillbox. Adjoining the B5031 road, N of **Rocester**. SK 105 400.

FW3/24 type pillbox. N of **Rocester**. SK 111 398.

Pillbox built as a railway station building at **Alton**, Staffs. SK 071 427.

Field gun emplacement disguised as a farm building at **Lower Ellastone,** Staffs. SK 120 425.

Pillbox on west bank of River Dove, near Birdgrove House, **Mayfield**, Staffs. SK 159 460.

Pillbox, Boat Inn, Basford Bridge Lane, **Cheddleton**, Staffordshire. Just about visible in a spinney in the pub garden by the side of the road. SJ 981 520.

Variant of FW3/26 type pillbox. Disguised as a cottage. By lane and former railway bridge, **Rudyard**, near Leek, Staffs. SJ 956 580.

FW3/24 type pillbox. Rear of the hotel car park, **Rudyard**. SJ 954 578.

The River Tern, Newport Canal and Shropshire Union Canal Line

Road block sockets, **Attingham Park**, near Shrewsbury. SJ 954 578.

FW3/22 type pillbox, **Upton Magna**, Shrops. SJ 559 113.

FW3/22 type pillbox, Duncote Farm, **Upton Magna**, Shrops. SJ 571 116.

FW3/24 type pillbox and cylinders. By canal bridge at Goldstone, **Cheswardine**, Shrops. SJ 705 294.

FW3/24 type pillbox. Newcastle Road, **Market Drayton**. By canal bridge where road crosses it. SJ 683 345.

FW3/24 type pillbox. Above canal and by A519, **Woodseaves**, Staffs. SJ 791 242.

FW3/22 type pillbox. Visible from road going S from **Edgmond**, Shropshire. SJ 718 184.

The Droitwich Junction Canal and Worcester and Birmingham Canal

Anti-tank cylinders, **Porters Mill,** N of Worcester. SO 861 602.

Stent pillbox, near **Droitwich Station** Signal Box. SO 895 637.

Anti-tank cylinders, Vines Lane, near Chapel Bridge, **Droitwich**, Worcs. SO 903 636.

Anti-tank cylinders, near Berry Mound, **Majors Green**, S of Solihull. They can be seen from a nearby public right of way. SP 099 778.

The Oxford Canal Stop Line to the S of Rugby

23 plus anti-tank cylinders, **Willoughby**, S of Rugby. SP 525 674.

Two anti-tank cylinders. At the entrance to **Wolfhamcote Hall**, Warwks. SP 526 653.

Two octagonal anti-tank blocks, **Napton on the Hill**, Warwks. SP 457 604.

Stent prefabricated pillbox, **Napton on the Hill**, Warwks. SP 458 603.

Stent prefabricated pillbox, Holt Farm, **Napton on the Hill**, Warwks. SP 459 596.

Two octagonal anti-tank blocks, near **Napton on the Hill**, Warwks. SP 459 594.

Stent prefabricated pillboxs, near **Priors Hardwick**, Warwks. SP 462 565, SP 458 548.

Six anti-tank cylinders, **Fenny Compton**, Warwks. SP 432 534.

Grand Union Canal East of Warwick

FW3/24 type pillbox. On a brick plinth constructed on the side of a railway embankment, **Radford Semele**, near Leamington. SP 353 649.

One octagonal anti-tank block. Near disused railway, near **Offchurch**, Warwickshire. SP 359 651.

Anti-Tank Islands and Nodal Points

Post-war development and redevelopment of urban areas has resulted in few defence structures surviving in urban areas. However, the following exist at the time of writing:

Birmingham Anti-Tank Island

FW3/25 type pillbox, disguised as a chimney, adjoining the Worcester and Birmingham Canal, Pershore Road (A441), Birmingham. Can be seen from canal towpath N of Pershore Road. SP 052 081.

FW3/26 type pillbox constructed on top of an industrial building. Gib Heath, Birmingham. The building is in the angle of the B4144 Villa Road and A41 Soho Hill. SP 053 892.

Burton on Trent Anti-Tank Island

Four small pillboxes. On railway bridge over River Trent. Visible from track on S bank. SK 245 210.

FW3/24 type pillbox. In water meadows opposite Tescos. SK 250 223.

Coventry Anti-Tank Island

Pillbox. Bennett's Road, Keresley, Coventry. Visible on side of road. SP 319 835.

Anti-tank cubes, Tile Hill, Coventry. SP 277 782.

Anti-tank cylinders, Devitts Green, NW of Coventry. SP 274 903.

Ellesmere, Shropshire, Anti-Tank Island

Anti-tank sockets, St John's Hill, Ellesmere. SJ 402 348.

Kidderminster Anti-Tank Island

Cable road block anchor point on the A442 near Shatterford. SO 799 804.

Cable road block anchor points on the unclassified Trimpley Road at Jacobs Ladder. SO 802 782.

Rugby Anti-Tank Island

Anti-tank pimples, Old Leicester Road. SP 503 771.

Anti-tank cylinders and vertical rails, Brownsover Lane. SP 509 776 and SP 510 776 respectively.

Stent pillbox, Clifton on Dunsmore, near Rugby. SP 523 758.

Shrewsbury Anti-Tank Island

Anti-tank sockets, corner of Underdale Road and Cleveland Street. SJ 502 128.

Loopholed wall, corner of Brook Street and Hereford Road. SJ 494 114.

Spigot Mortar pedestal, Shrewsbury Cemetery. SJ 487 111.

Spigot Mortar pedestal, Ellesmere Road, Greenlands. SJ 493 139.

Stafford Anti-Tank Island

FW3/26 type pillbox, adjacent to Baswich road bridge. SJ 945 225.

Tamworth Anti-Tank Island

Converted dovecote, Alvecote Priory, north-east of Tamworth. SK 251 043.

FW3/24 type pillbox in parkland, SW of Lady Bridge. SK 204 037.

Warwick/Leamington Anti-Tank Island

Octagonal road blocks, near Offchurch, E of Leamington. SP 382 666 and SP 359 651.

Isolated Defence Positions

Loopholed walls at the junction of an unclassified road and the B4031 road in the centre of **Fairfield**, near Bromsgrove, Worcestershire. SO 948 750.

Loopholed outbuilding, adjoining the Catholic Church, N of **Hanley Swan**, Worcs. SO 813 437.

Cable road block anchor points and flame fougasse housing in the rock cutting near **Dunley**, Worcs. SO 785 695.

Loopholed barn, can be seen from nearby lane at **Overton**, near Ludlow, Shrops. SO 504 721.

Defence of Vulnerable Points

Blackpole ROF, Worcester. One of three surviving Worcester Fortlets, formerly protecting the Blackpole ROF, can be seen on Perdiswell Golf Course. SO 861 580.

Rotherwas ROF, Hereford. Police post, on the main B4399 road. SO 537 378. Loopholed air raid shelters. SO 525 383 and SO 525 380. FW3/26 type pillbox, adjoining a public right of way. SO 483 350.

Summerfield ROF, Kidderminster. One of five surviving double-decked, FW3/26 type shellproof pillboxes can be seen from a nearby lane, SO 833 730 and another alongside the A449, SO 839 738.

Defence of Airfields

Atcham Airfield, Shrops. Oakington (FC Construction) pillbox, Uckington Farm. SJ 537 098. Seagull Trench, by track. SJ 578 102.

Baginton Airfield, Warwks. Battle headquarters. SP 344 741.

Bramcote Airfield, Warwks. Variant of FW3/26 type pillboxes. SP 417 876, SP 418 875, and SP 405 869.

Church Lawford Airfield, Warwks. FW3/22 type pillbox. SP 454 729. FW3/24 type pillbox. SP 455 735.

Cosford Airfield and Museum, Shrops. Yarnold Sangar (a modern version of the Norcon pillbox). Adjoining the museum. SJ 788 052. Rectangular pillbox on the side of the railway embankment and the museum entrance road. SJ 798 053.

Elmdon Airfield, Warwks. Battle headquarters adjacent to Birmingham Airport on opposite side of A45 Coventry Road near to Goodway Road. SP 164 836.

Halfpenny Green Airfield, Shrops. Pillbox in NE corner of the airfield at Bobbington, near Bridgnorth. SO 823 917. Pillbox in the SW corner of the airfield. SO 829 906. Pillbox at N end of the N/S runway. SO 822 916.

High Ercall Airfield, Shrops. Type FW3/26, shellproof pillbox built into the corner of a K-type hangar on the former technical site. SJ 603 187. Two camouflaged, rectangular pillboxes built to resemble a farm building, near the entrance to the airfield. SJ 598 188 and SJ 597 178.

Honeybourne Airfield, Worcs. Blast shelter on the former technical site. SP 117 424. A number of blast shelters on the former communal site. SP 122 417. Note: blast shelters had a dual role and could be used as defensive positions as well as protection of personnel from bombing attacks.

Lichfield Airfield

Pillbox to E of the A38 at Arlewas. SK 153 117. Pillbox on open land to SE of the airfield. SK 150 121. Pillbox to W of the airfield at Little Lyntus. SK 135 129. FW3/22 type pillbox on airfield approach road over the canal. SK 146 136.

Long Marston Airfield, Warwks. Battle headquarters; access can be gained via the trading estate. SP 175 494. Three Oakington (FC Construction) pillboxes; access again via the trading estate. SP 175 494.

Perdiswell Airfield, Worcester. Small guard post on bridge over canal from Friesland Close. SO 871 577.

Pershore Airfield, Worcs. FW3/22 type pillbox to W of Pershore Airfield. SO 963 501.

Rednal Airfield, Shrops. Three square pillboxes grouped around farm buildings at Haughton, near West Felton. SJ 373 271.

Shawbury Airfield, Shrops. FW3/27 type pillbox by lane to E of Lea Acton Farm. SJ 545 229. FW3/27 type pillbox at side of wood from B5063, to E of the airfield. SJ 560 224.

Stratford Airfield, Warwks. Two FW3/24 type pillboxes. SP 219 513 and SP 212 520.

Wellesbourne Airfield, Warwks. Battle headquarters now part of the Aviation Museum SP 265 545.

Chapter 7

The Shropshire Regimental Museum, The Castle, Shrewsbury, has a display concerning the county's Home Guard. Tel 01743 358516 for museum opening hours.

Chapter 8

Royal Observer Corps
(Full information on the country's ROC structures is available on the website of Subterranea Britannica www.subbrit.org.uk)

Group Headquarters
ROC headquarters (No 16 Group), Shrewsbury. Holywell Street, Shrewsbury (now a veterinary practice). SJ 500 126.

Underground monitoring posts
Herefordshire
Fownhope. On S side of the B4224 close to a lay-by. SO 592 340.

Pencombe. On a low mound 20 yards W of a minor road and 100 yards S of the entrance to Winslow Farm. SO 179 531.

Peterchurch. On Stockley Hill, on the east side of a bridleway. SO 362 393.

Shropshire
Hazler Hill, Church Stretton. On the summit, accessible via the rough track off the Church Stretton to Hope Bowdler road. SJ 465 929.

Market Drayton. By minor lane from the town to Longslow, just north of the by-pass. SJ 662 346.

Staffordshire
Rushton Spencer. Visible from public footpath following lane over Wormhill. SJ 940 633.

Silverdale. In High Lane, overlooking Silverdale colliery. SJ 815 477.

Standen. By minor lane SW of Standon village. SJ 818 344.

Warwickshire
Bidford-on-Avon. By footpath running by Bidford Grange golf course. SP 521 111.

Wolston. Viewable from Dyers Lane. SP 419 746.

Meriden. By the Showell Lane / A45 slip road junction. SP 262 825.

Worcestershire
Broadway. Buckle Street, next to a public footpath leading to Broadway Tower. SP 115 364.

Ombersley. School Bank, visible from public footpath near by-pass. SO 848 637.

Powick. Visible from a public footpath across the Hams. SO 828 519.

Redditch. Lowan's Hill Farm, Hewell Road. Post exposed by gravel workings, visible from the A441. SP 034 689.

Mobilisation Depots
Elson, Shrops. Large depot 2 miles NW of Ellesmere by B5068. SJ 384 358.

Tern Hill, Market Drayton, Shrops. Small depot situated off A41 and opposite Tern Hill barracks and airfield. SJ 643 318.

LAA defences
Hartlebury Common, Worcs. Light anti-aircraft earthworks visible. SO 824 707.

HAA defences

Wythall, Crabmill Lane. Radar plinth of former HAA battery visible from public footpath. SP 071 781

Bannerhill, Kenilworth, Warwks. HAA battery (gun pits and command post) adjacent to footpath and farm road near Goodrest Farm, Rouncil Lane, near Kenilworth. SP 275 693.

Fillongley, Warwks. HAA gun battery near High House Farm, visible from Breach Oak Lane, 1 mile E of Fillongley. SP 301 871.

Birmingham, The Uplands. Remains of HAA battery, accessible from footpath running directly from Silvercroft Avenue, Handsworth. SP 036 913.

Radar station

RAF Comberton GCI station ('Happidrome'), Wick, Worcs. Buildings visible from the road off the B4084 to Glenmore Farm. SO 967 461.

Decoy sites with remaining structures
Shropshire

Haughmond Hill, near Shrewsbury. Two decoy control bunkers on hillock, visible from extreme eastern edge of Forestry Commission wood (public access). SJ 549 142.

Staffordshire

Beech. Bunker in NW corner of a small wood, by public path. SJ 851 375.

Whittington. Site visible from a track off a minor road heading E from Whittington village. Decoy bunker at SO 864 832.

Warwickshire

Pillerton Priors. Decoy site 1 mile NE of the village, bunker at SP 309 480. ('Q' decoy for RAF Wellesbourne.)

Hunningham. Decoy site 1 mile SW of the village, bunker by a bridleway. SP 364 672.

Bretford. Site ¾mile W of the village, bunker at SP 418 777.

Meriden, Coventry. Site 1½ miles NE of Meriden, bunker at SP 275 833.

Wibtoft. Site 1 mile S of the village, bunker at SP 468 864.

Worcestershire

Brockamin, near Leigh, Worcester. Bunker can be seen on W side of lane that extends beyond Dingle Road, a couple of fields beyond the last house. SO 772 541.

Hunnington near Halesowen: Bunker can be seen from public footpath by Goodrest Farm, off the B4551. SO 970 815.

Netherton. By public footpath running off Smokey Lane, which is off the B4084, bunker at SO 999 429.

Chapter 9

Air Raid Shelters
i) Anderson Shelter

A reconstructed Anderson shelter can be seen in the grounds of the **Staffordshire Regiment Museum**, Whittington Barracks, Whittington, near Lichfield. SK 154 065.

ii) Surface Domestic Shelters

Croome Park (a National Trust property), near Defford, Worcs. A brick shelter can be seen by the public car park of this property near other Second World War buildings of RAF, Defford. SO 890 445.

Government Buildings, Whittington Road, **Worcester**. A brick shelter can be seen just inside the entrance to the site. SO 872 536.

Brook Street, **Worcester**. At the end of Brook Street is a shelter in the grounds of St George's Primary School. SO 8475 5631.

Stourport Road, Wribbenhall, **Bewdley**, Worcs. Large communal shelter on side of road in grounds of Wribbenhall Middle School. SO 794 751.

Elm Place, **Cookley**, Worcs. A large communal shelter can be seen just off Elm Place. It still bears a large 'S' sign indicating 'shelter here'. SO 8456 7998.

Primary School, School Lane, **Hopwas**, Staffs. The shelter can be seen from the canal towpath when heading N from the A51 road bridge. SK 180 052.

School Lane, **Alvechurch**, Worcs. A shelter can be seen behind the wooden hut of the local history society which is off School Lane. SP 028 722.

Adams Grammar School, High Street, **Newport**, Shrops. A shelter can be seen in the school grounds. SJ 743 192

Chester Road North, **Kidderminster**, Worcs. A shelter can be seen on the E side of the road near the junction with Hurcott Road. SO 8406 7758.

South Road, **Clifton upon Dunsmore**, Warwks. Shelter opposite village school. SP 528 762.

Church Street, **Clifton upon Dunsmore**, Warwks. Shelter on W side of road. SP 531 764.

iii) Stanton Shelters

Petrol depot, **Ripple**, near Upton-on-Severn. A Stanton shelter can be seen on the site which can be seen from public footpaths near to the River Severn. SO 864 395.

B4362, Stratford Road, near **Weston-Sub-Edge**, Gloucs. Several Stanton shelters can be seen in a field on SE side of this road. SP 131 415. (Note: Although in Gloucs. these shelters were part of the RAF Honeybourne complex which was mainly in Worcs.)

Welsh Road, **Southam**, Warwks. Shelter can be seen at far end of allotments on edge of Southam. SP 425 613.

Shipston Road (A3400), **Atherstone-on-Stour,** Warwks. The remains of a Stanton can be seen in the small wood on SE side of crossroads at Ailstone. SP 211 512.

Campden Road (B4632), **Long Marston**, Warwks. A Stanton can be seen from the lane to Wincot Farm. It is behind the first group of buildings on S side of the lane. SP 180 492.

Kingstone, Herefs. A Stanton can be seen just inside the entrance to the playing field. SO 426 361.

Sutton Road, near **Market Drayton**. Stantons can be seen in a field to S of this road. SJ 657 315.

Cold War Sites

RSG, Drakelow, near Kidderminster. Very little can be seen as the complex is underground. The entrance can be seen from Drakelow Lane. SO 823 811.

Microwave Tower, Pye Green, **Cannock**, Staffs. The tower can be from the Green and Brindley Road. SJ 988 144.

Microwave Tower, Winwood Heath Road, **Romsley**, Worcs. The tower is clearly visible from this road, other roads nearby and the N Worcs. Footpath. SO 961 786.

Microwave Tower, **The Wrekin**, Shrops. This tower is clearly visible from surrounding roads. SJ 628 083.

Microwave Tower, Lionel Street, **Birmingham**. Tower can clearly be seen from streets in city centre. SP 066 872.

Repeater Station, Whitecrest, off Queslett Road, **Sandwell**. Building can clearly be seen near to the junction of these two roads. SP 052 943.

Repeater Station, New Coventry Road, **Birmingham**. The station is located on the island formed by the divergence of the Coventry Road and the New Coventry Road. It can be seen from both roads. SP141 842.

Fire Services

NFS HQ, Bevere Manor, near Worcester. Manor can be seen at the end of Bevere Lane and from footpath along river bank. SO 841 594.

NFS HQ, **Pirehill House**, off A34, near Stone, Staffs. Can be seen from nearby footpath. SO 841 594.

AFS/NFS Fire Station, Teme Street, **Tenbury Wells**, Worcs. On the east side of the street almost next to the river bridge. SO 5958 6852.

Fire Station, Copenhagen Street/Deansway, **Worcester**. A good example of a late 1930s fire station. SO 8494 5474.

Water Tank, St Godwalds Road, **Bromsgrove**. The remains of a large circular concrete water tank can be seen on the east side of the road by a row of houses. SO 970 693.

Chapter 10

Principal airfields where there are significant or substantial remains together with some public access, or where it is possible to see some remains from roads and public footpaths. However, some are still in military use and these are indicated. The RAF Museum at Hendon in London has wartime plans for purchase of many of the airfields listed below: www.rafmuseum.org.uk.

Herefordshire
Madley. 6 miles WSW of Hereford. SO 420 375.

Shobdon. On the minor road from B4362 at Shobdon village. SO 395 605.

Shropshire
Cosford. By the A41 just south of its junction with the M54. The exhibits of the Aerospace Museum are in former RAF hangars, whilst many of the buildings currently used by the RAF are visible from the museum. The National Cold War Museum is also on the site: www.rafmuseum.org.uk and www.nationalcoldwarexhibition.org.uk. SJ 790 045. Visible from a minor lane running from the A41 to north of the airfield is the monumental 1930s RAF Fulton Block barracks. SJ 793 058.

High Ercall. By B5062 1 mile W of Crudgington. SJ 605 185.

Hinstock. 1 mile NW of Childs Ercall by an unclassified road. SJ 660 260.

Monkmoor (First World War). On the NE outskirts of Shrewsbury. SJ 512 135.

Montford Bridge. 1 mile N of the village by an unclassified road. SJ 435 170.

Peplow. Just S of Childs Ercall on the minor road to Sutton-upon-Tern. SJ 660 235.

Rednal. 1½ miles NE of the A5 by the West Felton. SJ 375 275.

Shawbury (still in military use). Between the A53 and B5063 close to Shawbury. SJ 550 220.

Sleap. Off the A5113, 2 miles N of Myddle. SJ 480 265.

Tern Hill (in military use by the Army as Clive Barracks). By the junction of the A53 and A41. SJ 645 310.

Tilstock. By the A41, 3 miles S of Whitchurch. SJ 560 375.

Staffordshire
Halfpenny Green. 3½ miles SW of Wombourne. SO 825 910.

Hixon. Between the A51 and A518, 3 miles N of Stafford. SJ 995 265.

Lichfield. By the A38 NE of Lichfield. SK 145 130.

Seighford. On the B5405 1½ miles SW of Great Bridgeford. SJ 865 255.

Warwickshire
Baginton (now Coventry Airport). 4 miles south east of Coventry. SP 362 745. The Midland Air Museum is located there as well as a number of Second World War hangars etc. www.midlandairmuseum.co.uk, telephone 02476 301033.

Bramcote (in military use by the Army as Gamecock Barracks). NE of Coventry, S of the B4114. SP 406 883.

Long Marston. 6 miles N of Chipping Camden by the A46. SP170 480.

Stratford. 3½ miles S of Stratford-upon-Avon. SP 215 515.

Wellesbourne Mountford. 5 miles E of Stratford-upon-Avon off the B4086. SP 265 548. There is a small museum here based around the former battle headquarters. www.welles-bourneairfield.com/museum 01789 778816.

Worcestershire
Honeybourne. 2 miles NW of Weston-sub-Edge by the A4035. SP 025 300.

Defford. 1 mile W of Defford. SO 900 440.

Pershore. By the B4082, 2 miles NE of Pershore. SO 975 495.

Chapter 11

Camps and depots
Cannock Chase. Fragmentary remains of the two large First World War camps are spread over the Chase: for further information contact the Cannock Chase Visitor Centre, Marquis Drive, Cannock Chase.

Whittington Barracks, Staffs. By the A51, 2 miles NW of Hopwas village. SK 154 068 (still in military use).

Shrewsbury. Copthorne Barracks, Copthorne Road. SJ 479 129 (still in military use).

Worcester. Norton Barracks (only the keep remains) on Norton Road 1 mile NW of the village of Norton. SO 868 518.

Gamecock Barracks (former Bramcote Airfield), Warwks. 3 miles SE of Nuneaton. SP 405 885 (still in military use).

Kineton Depot, Warwks. 3.5 miles E of Kineton village, on both sides of the B4086. SP 375 515 (still in military use).

Long Marston Depot, Warwks. 5 miles SE of Stratford-upon-Avon. SP 160 470.

Drill Halls
Herefordshire
Hereford. Harold Street. Former militia barracks, now the County Record Office. SO 518 394. Also see entry in the Gazetteer, Chapter 13, Belgian forces.

Leominster. New Street. 1960s TA Centre, still in use as such. SO 494 592.

Ross-on-Wye. Alton Road. Former drill hall from the 1930s. SO 607 240.

Shropshire
Ironbridge. St Lukes Road. Former early nineteenth-century armoury. SJ 674 034.

Shrewsbury. Coleham. Former drill hall of 1865. SJ 496 122.

Shrewsbury. Sundorne Road. 1930s Territorial Army centre, still in use as such. SJ 512 147.

Staffordshire
Burslem. Newcastle Street. Drill hall of 1902. Smethwick, Broomfield. Former pre-First World War drill hall. SP 019 883.

Stafford. Newport Street. Early twentieth-century drill hall. SJ 921 228.

Tamworth. Corporation Street. Drill hall of 1911. SK 205 042.

Walsall. Whittimere Street. Drill hall of 1910. SK 016 087.

Birmingham
Harborne. Tennal Grange. In use as an OTC and Reserve Force and Cadet Association HQ. SP 022 842

Sparkbrook. Golden Hillock Road. Drill hall of 1930s still in use by TA. SP 096 845

City Centre. Thorp Street. Drill hall, pre-1880. SP 070 863.

Warwickshire
Coventry. Radford Road. Built in 1990s as a TA Centre. SP 328 802.

Rugby. Edward Street. Pre-First World War drill hall. SP 497 756.

Stratford. New Broad Street. Former drill hall of the 1930s.

Warwick. St Johns. Former pre-First World War drill hall. SP 289 653.

Worcestershire
Bromsgrove. Recreation Road. Early twentieth-century drill hall. SO 959 710.

Evesham. Bengeworth, Coronation Street. Pre-First World War drill hall, now a social club. SP 047 437.

Pershore. Defford Road. Pre-First World War drill hall, now a fire station. SO 947 454.

Tenbury Wells. Berrington Road. Early twentieth-century drill hall, now in use as a police station. SO 594 681.

Chapter 12

Guard accommodation huts for the former Admiralty Store in the railway tunnel through the Malvern Hills can still be seen off Peachfield Road, **Great Malvern**, Worcestershire, at SO 779 442, and to the rear of Colwall Station, Herefordshire, at SO 757 424.

The former HMS Duke (now occupied by Qinetiq) retains a few of the original buildings at St Andrews Road, **Great Malvern**. SO 785 447.

The former HMS Daedalus headquarters at Clayton Hall, **Newcastle under Lyme**, Staffs. SJ 835 435.

The former Fleet Air Arm air station, HMS Godwit at **Hinstock**, near Childs Ercall, Shrops. SJ 660 260.

Chapter 13

American Forces

Fighter pilot ETO training, **Atcham Airfield**, near Shrewsbury. SJ 570 105.

The remains of a small former US Ranger camp, adjoining the railway station at **Leominster**, Herefordshire. SO 502 589.

Honeybourne Depot, near Evesham, Worcestershire. This is occupied by Unipart but can be seen from adjoining roads. SP 093 452.

Ashchurch Depot, near Tewkesbury and adjoining the regional boundary. This is still in use by the Army Logistical Corps but can be seen from adjoining roads. SO 938 339.

Wem, Shrops. (Site of US 83rd Ordnance Sub Depot), Romney huts now used as a trading estate, by the B5065 on the E side of the town. SJ 525 300.

ANZAC Forces

Australian and New Zealand Air Force aircrew trained at No 27 OTU based at **Lichfield Airfield**, Staffs. SK 145 130.

Belgian Forces

Belgian Army HQ 1941/42, The Abbey Hotel, Priory Road, **Great Malvern**. SO 776 458.

Belgian Forces, The Old Barracks (now the Herefordshire County Record Office), Harold Street, **Hereford**. SO 518 394.

Canadian Forces

Canadian Air Force personnel trained with No 23 OTU based at **Pershore Airfield**, Worcs., SO 975 495, and with No 81 OTU based at **Tilstock Airfield**, Shrops., SJ 603 375.

Czech Forces

Czech forces were located in the Leamington Spa area from October 1940 till May 1942. As well as the following locations the brigade were based at Barford Hill, Butlers Marston, Friz Hill, Kineton, Leamington Spa and Moreton Paddox. Independent Czech Brigade, **Moreton Hall**, Moreton Morrell, Warwickshire. SP 305 555, and **Walton Hall**, near Wellesbourne, Warwks. SP 285 524.

Czech Forces Memorial, Jephson Gardens, **Leamington Spa**, Warwks. SP 320 657.

Czech Air Force personnel trained at the No 2 Technical Training School, **Cosford**, near Wolverhampton. SJ 790 045.

Free French Forces

Cadets de la France Libre OCTU 1941/42, No 5 House, **Malvern College**. SO 779 453.

Cadets de la France Libre OCTU 1942/44, **Ribbesford House**, near Bewdley. SO 787 738.

Post-Dunkirk French Forces, Trentham Gardens, **Stoke on Trent**, Staffs. SJ 860 410.

Polish Forces

Polish Carpathian Chasseurs, Trentham Gardens, **Stoke on Trent**, Staffs. SJ 860 410.

Polish Air Force personnel trained at RAF No 2 Technical Training School, **Cosford**, near Wolverhampton. SJ 790 045. Also at RAF Hereford, **Credenhill**, Herefs. SO 455 432.

Polish Air Force Operational Training Unit, **RAF Bramcote**, Warwks. SP 406 883.

No 308 Fighter Squadron was based at **Baginton Airfield** (now Coventry Airport). SP 355 745.

Chapter 14

The Barracks, **Shelsley Walsh**, Worcs. These were a First World War PoW camp and can be seen opposite the entrance to Shelsley Walsh Hill Climb. SO 722 632.

Moors Bank, (B5070), St Martins, Shrops. The substantial remains of this Second World War PoW camp are now an industrial estate. SJ 311 363.

Acksea Farm, Edgerley, Shrop. The site of this Second World War PoW camp is now a military training area but the remains of the camp can be seen from public footpaths crossing the area. SJ 354 194.

Somerford Hall, Brewood, Staffs. This First World War PoW camp for officers can be viewed from its long approach road. SJ 900 082.

Recreation Ground, Long Hyde Road, **South Littleton**, Worcs. On the far side of the ground is the last remaining hut from a Second World War PoW camp. SP 075 462.

Loxley Hall, Stafford Road (A518), near Uttoxeter. Used in Second World War as a PoW camp the Hall is now a Special School and is about 2 miles from Uttoxeter. SK 062 321.

Davenport House, Worfield, Shrops. The house was used as a Second World War PoW camp and is off the minor road bypassing Worfield. SO 753 954.

Hillhampton House, A443, near Great Witley, Worcs. Used in First World War as a PoW camp, the house can be seen across the road from the entrance to Witley Court. SO 775 654.

Radbourne Lane, **Ladbroke**, Warwks. One concrete hut and two Nissens, all that remain of a Second World War PoW camp, can be seen from this lane. SP 421 586.

Chapter 15

Cemeteries
Commonwealth War Graves Commission and German Cemeteries, near Brindley Heath, **Cannock Chase**. SJ 983 155.

Canadian and other Air Force casualties at Evesham Cemetery, Waterside, **Evesham**. SP 037 432.

Canadian and other Air Force casualties at Pershore Cemetery, Defford Road, **Pershore**. SO 937 454.

First World War Hospitals
Birmingham and Black Country
Birmingham University (1st Southern Hospital), University Hall and other buildings, Edgbaston. SP 048 835.

Lightwoods House, Adkins Lane, Smethwick. SP 020 860.

The Old Manor House, Wightwick Bank, Wolverhampton. A National Trust property. SO 869 985.

Harborne Hall, Church Road, Harborne, Birmingham. Now a training centre. SP 030 839.

The Beeches, Selly Oak Road, Bourneville. Now a conference centre. SP 041 808.

The Grange, Halesowen. Grange Hill. Now a sports club. SO 971 828.

Highbury, 4 Yew Tree Road, Moseley. Now a conference and banqueting centre. SP 067 826.

Herefordshire
Brand Lodge, Jubilee Drive, Brand Green, Colwall. SO 766 412.

Shropshire
Aston Hall, Aston on Clun. Hall is marked on OS maps. SO 391 817.

Hodnet Hall, Hodnet, near Market Drayton. Occasionally open to public. SJ 610 285.

Attingham Park, near Shrewsbury. A National Trust property. SJ 550 099.

Peplow Hall, Market Drayton. Visible from lane. SJ 639 247.

Pell Wall Hall, near Market Drayton. Visible from A529 Market Drayton to Hinstock road. SJ 676 331.

Warwickshire
Longbridge Manor, Stratford Road (A429), Longbridge, near Warwick. Now a company headquarters. SP 267 625.

Old Manor, Queen Street, Halford, Shipston on Stour. Now a hotel. SP 260 456.

Maxstoke Castle, near Coleshill. Occasionally open to public. SK 226 892.

Worcestershire
Abbey Manor, The Squires, Evesham. Just visible from road. SP 033 457.

Kyrewood House, B4204, near Tenbury. Visible from road. SO 604 677.

The Boynes, near Upton upon Severn. Now a nursing home. SO 831 406.

Hartlebury Castle, near Kidderminster. Next to County Museum. SO 837 712.

Rhydd Court, B4211, Hanley Castle. Now Alps College. Buildings can be glimpsed through roadside trees. SO 837 450

Second World War Hospitals
Herefordshire
Berrington Hall, near Leominster. A National Trust property. SO 509 637.

Homme House, Much Marcle. A private house licensed for weddings. SO 654 318.

Bosbury House, Bosbury, near Ledbury. On B4220 NE of Bosbury. SO 709 439.

Shropshire
Ashford Hall, Ashford Bowdler, Ludlow. Visible from lane. SO 513 712.

Brogyntyn, Oswestry. Visible from lane. SJ 272 311.

Childs Ercall. Visible from lane. SJ 665 254.

Longmynd Hotel, off Ludlow Road (B4370), Church Stretton. On lane going uphill from B4370. SO 449 934.

Staffordshire
Longdon Hall, Rugely. Visible from A51. SK 083 138.

Rodbaston, A449, near Penkridge. Now an agricultural college. SJ 920 115.

Thorpe Hall, Tamworth. Visible from village. SK 258 090.

Warwickshire
Bilton House, 5 Bawnmore Road, Rugby. Now an old peoples' home. SP486 737.

Ragley Hall, off A435, near Alcester. Open to the public. SP 073 556.

Shuckburgh Park, A425, Near Napton on the Hill. Viewable from road to Upper Shuckburgh. SP 497 619.

Worcestershire
Evesham Emergency Hospital, Waterside (B4035). Now the town's Community Hospital. SP 037 430.

Kyrewood House, B4204, near Tenbury Wells. Visible from road. SO 604 680.

Powick Asylum, off Malvern Road (A449), Powick, near Worcester. The main block, now called Barrington Grange, has been retained as part of a housing development and can be seen at the end of Harrison Close. SO 8203 5062.

American Hospitals
Herefordshire
Kington Camp, Mahollam, near Kington. There are still a few huts left within an industrial estate but the main surviving feature is a massive brick water tower. SO 274 544.

Shropshire
Shugborough Park, Milford, near Stafford. There are still one or two hospital huts in the park. SJ 995 215.

Warwickshire
Stoneleigh Convalescent Hospital, near Kenilworth. A number of huts remain in the Deer Park. Some can be seen from the Stareton road off the B4113. SP 340 717.

Worcestershire
Blackmore No 1 Camp, Poolbrook, near Malvern. A number of hospital ward huts and two large brick water towers remain within a small trading estate which is off the E side of Poolbrook Road. SO 799 436.

Blackmore No 2 Camp, Blackmore End, near Hanley Swan. Two ward huts remain within a camping site off the minor road N of Hanley Swan. SO 812 443.

Merebrook Camp, Hanley Road, near Hanley Swan. A number of huts remain within a trading estate on the S side of the road. SO 799 425. The officers' mess remains at SO 795 424.

Wolverley Camp, Wolverley Road, near Kidderminster. A few ward buildings remain within a sports complex and camping site on the N side of the road near the River Stour. SO 834 792.

BIBLIOGRAPHY

ALANBROOKE, Lord. *War Diaries 1939-1945.* London, 2001.

ALEXANDER, C. *Ironside's Line.* Storrington, West Sussex, 1999.

ANON. *Reports by the Joint War Committee and the Joint War Finance Committee of the British Red Cross and the Order of St John of Jerusalem in England.* London, 1921.

ANON. *Army Camps: History and Development, 1858-2000.* Undated report commissioned by English Heritage.

ANON. *Britain's Modern Army Illustrated.* London, no date but c.1940s.

ANON. *Ourselves in Wartime.* London, no date but c.1940s.

ANON. *Shropshire's War.* Shrewsbury, 2005.

BEBBINGTON, G. *Trentham at War.* Leek, 1995.

BEBBINGTON, G. *Ship without Water.* Leek, 1999.

BLACKSTONE, G.V. *A History of the British Fire Service.* London, 1957.

BOWYER, M. J. F. *Action Stations 6 – Military airfields of Cotswolds and Central Midlands.* Wellingborough, 1983.

BRAZIER, R H & SANDFORD, E. *Birmingham and the Great War.* Birmingham, 1921.

BREW, A. *History of Black Country Aviation.* Stroud, 1993.

BREW, A. *RAF Cosford in Old Photographs.* Stroud, 1995.

BREW, A. *Staffordshire and Black Country Airfields.* Stroud, 1997.

BRIGGS, A. *History of Broadcasting in the United Kingdom.* 5 volumes. Oxford, 1961-95.

BURRIDGE, D. *20th Century Defences in Britain – Kent.* London, 1997.

CALDER, A. *The People's War.* London, 1969.

CAMBRAY, P.G. & BRIGGS, G.G.B. *Red Cross and St John War History, 1939-1947.* London, 1949.

CAMPBELL, D. *War Plan UK.* London, 1982.

CARVELL, S. *Twentieth Century Defences in Warwickshire.* Stroud, 2007.

COCROFT, W. & THOMAS, R. *Cold War.* Swindon, 2003.

COCROFT, W. *Dangerous Energy.* Swindon, 2000.

COLLIER, B. *The Defence of the United Kingdom.* London, 1957.

COLLINS, F. & M. *Camp Foxley.* Studley, Warwickshire, 2005.

COLLINS, F. & M. *They Also Serve Who Stand and Wait: A History of Pheasey Farms US Army Replacement Depot 1943/1945.* Studley, 2001.

COLLINS, M. & F. *Letters for Victory.* Studley, 1993.

COLLINS, F. & M. *Somewhere in the Midlands: A History of USAAF Station 522, Smethwick.* Studley, 1998.

COOKSLEY, P. *The Home Front.* Stroud, 2006.

DE GAULLE, C. *The Call to Honour.* London, 1955.

DOBINSON, C. *AA Command.* London, 2001.

DOBINSON, C. *Fields of Deception: Britain's Bombing Decoys of WW2.* London, 2000.

DOUGLAS, A. *Coventry at War.* Studley, 2003.

DOUGLAS, A. *Birmingham at War.* Birmingham, 1982.

DOUGLAS, A. Birmingham at War (vol. 2). Birmingham no date.

EDMONDS, J. *The History of Rotherwas Munitions Factory, Hereford.* Logaston, Herefordshire, 2004.

FEGAN, T. *The 'Baby Killers'*. Barnsley, 2002.

FOOT, W. *Beaches, fields, streets and hills*. York, 2006.

FRANCIS, P. *British Military Airfield Architecture*. Yeovil, 1996.

GARDINER, J. *Wartime Britain 1939-1945*. London, 2004.

GAUNT, H.C.A. *Two Exiles - A School in Wartime*. London, 1946.

GILLMAN, P. & L. *Collar the Lot*. London, 1980.

GRIFFIN, A. *Leamington's Czech Patriots and the Heydrich Assassination*. No address, 2004.

HALPENNY, B.B. *Action Stations 2: Military Airfields of Lincolnshire and the East Midlands*. Wellingborough, 1981.

HARTCUP, G. *The Challenge of War*. Newton Abbot, 1970.

HIGGINBOTHAM, J. *Kington Camp*. Kington, Herefordshire, 1980.

HORNBY, W. *Factories and Plant*. London, 1958.

JONES, R.V. *Most Secret War*. London, 1978.

KNIGHT. T.J. *The Fort on the Hill: The Story of RAF Hereford*. Privately published, no date.

KNOWLES, N. *De Gaulle and the Free French in Bewdley, 1942-44*. Bewdley, Worcs., 1999.

LAMPE, D. *The Last Ditch*. London, 1968.

LISIEWICZ, M (ed). *Destiny Can Wait*. London, 1949.

LONGMATE, N. *Air Raid: The Bombing of Coventry, 1940*. London, 1976.

LOVELL, Sir Bernard. *Echoes of War – The Story of H2S Radar*. Bristol, 1991.

LOWRY, B. *British Home Defences, 1940-45*. Oxford, 2004.

LOWRY, B. & WILKS, M. *The Mercian Maquis*. Logaston, Herefordshire, 2002.

MacKENZIE, S.P. *The Home Guard*. Oxford, 1995.

MACKLIN, F. *The Story of RAF Madley*. Logaston, 2007.

McCAMLEY, N.J. *Cold War Secret Nuclear Bunkers*. Barnsley, 2002.

McCAMLEY, N.J. *Saving Britain's Art Treasures*. Barnsley, 2003.

McCAMLEY, N.J. *Secret Underground Cities*. Barnsley, 1998.

MELLY, G. *Rum, Bum and Concertina*. London, 1977.

MOORE, B & FEDOROWICH, K. *Prisoners of War and their Captors in World War 2*. London, 1996

MORRAH, D. *The British Red Cross*. London, 1944.

NATIONAL ARCHIVES. Various documents in the WO166/ and WO199/ series.

NEAL, T. *Shropshire Airfields*. Telford, 2005.

NORTH, J., MORAN, M., and BARTON, J. *The Old Rectory Whitchurch, Shropshire*. Logaston, Herefordshire, 2007.

O'BRIEN, T.H. *Civil Defence*. London, 1955.

OSBORNE, M. *Defending Britain*. Stroud, 2004.

OSBORNE, M. *Always Ready: The Drill Halls of Britain's Volunteer Forces*. Leigh-on-Sea, 2006.

OSBORNE, M. *Pillboxes of Britain and Ireland*. Stroud, 2007.

PRICE, A. *Blitz on Britain 1939-1945*. Abingdon, 1977.

PRISONERS OF WAR INFORMATION BUREAU. *Lists of Places of Internment*. London, 1919.

RENIER, O and RUBINSTEIN, V. *Assigned to Listen*. BBC, 1986.

ROBINSON, M. *The Country House at War*. London, 1989.

REYNOLDS, D. *Rich Relations*. London, 1995.

SACKVILLE-WEST, V. *The Women's Land Army*. London, 1944.

SANDERS, I.J. *Pillboxes*. Privately published, 2005.

SCARTH, R.N. *Echoes from the Sky*. Hythe Civic Society, 1999.

SEBAG-MONTEFIORE, H. *Dunkirk – Fight to the Last Man*. London, 2006.

SMITH, D. J. *Action Stations 3 – Military airfields of Wales and North West*. Cambridge, 1981.

TAYLOR, E. *Wartime Nurse*. London, 2001.

THOMAS, R. *Prisoner of War Camps*. English Heritage, Swindon, 2003. (Published on EH internet site.)

TURLEY, A. & N. *Camp Bewdley*. Bewdley, Worcs, 2000.

TURLEY, A. & N. *The US Army in South East Shropshire 1944*. Kidderminster, 2004.

TWINCH, C. *Women on the Land*. Cambridge, 1990.

WAKEFIELD, K. *Operation Bolero*. Crecy Books, 1994.

WHITEHOUSE, C.J. & G.P. *A Town for Four Winters: Great War camps on Cannock Chase*. Privately published, 1983.

WILKS, M. *The Defence of Worcestershire*. Logaston, Herefordshire, 2007.

WILLS, H. *Pillboxes*. London, 1985.

WOOD, D. *Attack Warning Red*. Portsmouth, 1992.

Index

Page numbers in italics refer to illustrations

Also from Logaston Press

The Defence of Worcestershire
and the southern approaches to Birmingham in World War II
by Mick Wilks

Paperback, 256 pages, with 150 black and white maps and photographs
ISBN 978 1904396 80 2   £14.95

In the summer of 1940, an invasion of Britain by the apparently invincible forces of the Third Reich was widely expected. In the time-honoured fashion of the British, preparations to meet the invasion were left almost to the last moment. This book tells the story of how Worcestershire was prepared for defence against both ground and air attack by the enemy. The county was the chosen location for both the Government and Royal Family had it been necessary to evacuate them from London, and the county occupies a crucial location on the southern approaches to Birmingham and the Black Country, whose industries were then busily producing aircraft and munitions. The opportunity is also taken in this volume to bring up to date the research into the covert forces recruited in the county (as otherwise covered in *The Mercian Maquis*, see below). After a career in town planning, but now retired and working as a part-time volunteer researcher with the Worcestershire History Environment and Archaeology Service, Mick Wilks has been researching and recording modern defence sites in Worcestershire for over 12 years.

The Mercian Maquis
by Bernard Lowry and Mick Wilks (2007 Reprint)

Paperback, 146 pp, with 70 black and white maps and photographs
ISBN 978 1 873827 97 0   £7.95

For decades after the end of the Second World War little was known about the secretive organisation known as the Auxiliary Units. Formed in 1940, at the same time as the Home Guard, its members were recruited from amongst a tightly-knit farming community and from those in other reserved occupations. Organised into patrols of about half a dozen men and knowing their locality intimately, their role would have been to carry out acts of sabotage and terror behind the German invader's lines. From carefully camouflaged underground Operational Bases liberally supplied with explosive and arms, patrols would have set out at night to harry the invader. Over a period of several years the authors have interviewed surviving patrol members and have found or identified Operational Bases throughout the two counties.